Inspired Learners, Active Minds

A Guide for the English Classroom

Dennis J. Kafalas

Rowman & Littlefield Education
Lanham • New York • Toronto • Plymouth, UK

Published in the United States of America
by Rowman & Littlefield Education
A Division of Rowman & Littlefield Publishers, Inc.
A wholly owned subsidiary of The Rowman & Littlefield Publishing Group, Inc.
4501 Forbes Boulevard, Suite 200, Lanham, Maryland 20706
www.rowmaneducation.com

Estover Road
Plymouth PL6 7PY
United Kingdom

Copyright © 2008 by Dennis K. Kafalas

All rights reserved. No part of this publication may be reproduced, stored in a retrieval system, or transmitted in any form or by any means, electronic, mechanical, photocopying, recording, or otherwise, without the prior permission of the publisher.

British Library Cataloguing in Publication Information Available

Library of Congress Cataloging-in-Publication Data

Kafalas, Dennis J., 1955–
  Inspired learners, active minds : a guide for the English classroom / Dennis J. Kafalas
     p.   cm.
  Includes bibliographical references
  ISBN-13: 978-1-57886-723-3 (cloth : alk. paper)
  ISBN-10: 1-57886-723-1 (cloth : alk. paper)
  ISBN-13: 978-1-57886-724-0 (pbk. : alk. paper)
  ISBN-10: 1-57886-724-X (pbk. : alk. paper)
  1. English language—Study and teaching (Middle school)—United States.
  2. English language—Study and teaching (Secondary)—United States. I. Title.
  LB1631.K22 2008
  428.0071'273—dc22   2007045938

∞^{TM} The paper used in this publication meets the minimum requirements of American National Standard for Information Sciences—Permanence of Paper for Printed Library Materials, ANSI/NISO Z39.48-1992.
Manufactured in the United States of America.

CONTENTS

Preface v

Introduction vii

    CHAPTER ONE Why Use Reading and
Writing Workshop? 1

    CHAPTER TWO Suspending Disbelief 3

    CHAPTER THREE First Step: Choice and Ownership
of Reading and Writing 5

    CHAPTER FOUR The Writer's Notebook 9

    CHAPTER FIVE The Writing Workshop 18

    CHAPTER SIX Grading 59

    CHAPTER SEVEN Bringing Literature
into the Classroom 66

    CHAPTER EIGHT Performance-Based Exams 87

    CHAPTER NINE Writing the Research Paper 96

CONTENTS

CHAPTER TEN Portfolios, Assessment,
and Metacognition 110

CHAPTER ELEVEN Starting the School Year
in the Workshop Model 118

Selected Bibliography 139

About the Author 143

Permissions 144

PREFACE

This book presents a manageable and successful teaching approach that is grounded in "best practice" and the latest research in Language Arts instruction. For the first time, teaching strategies that work with all students, and that are quantifiable through data-based research and classroom evidence, are available to teachers as best practice. The classroom methodology presented here—the workshop model—is a blend of the research and practice of other scholars. I am indebted to their fine work and credit them wherever possible.

I have synthesized these strategies into a portfolio-based Language Arts class methodology that is easy to use and raises expectations for thinking, learning, and writing. It is also a practical way in which to engage students to try their best and approach learning to be successful.

A number of models and guides are provided to the reader that can serve as a basis for the classroom, but they are by no means meant to be the only way to proceed. The true beauty of a workshop class is how it is adaptable to any instructor's style or to the unique makeup of any student group, and while the reader can certainly use the materials provided, over time teachers can personalize their

PREFACE

approach in the spirit that a student-centered workshop class intends and requires.

To best use this book, read it through first—although one could go to an individual chapter to use the materials there—because much of the planning and management of a reading-and-writing workshop class builds from a day-to-day understanding of the internal design that a class like this needs to be successful.

INTRODUCTION

While we all understand the sentiment of No Child Left Behind, putting a classroom model in place that personalizes learning to the point where *all* students develop meaningful skills is the ultimate challenge. Many argue, however, that this individualized approach is idealistic and unrealistic.

Although best practice has been defined for teachers in writing and reading, they struggle with the transition from a traditional, content-focused classroom to one that uses best practice exclusively.

More often than not, teachers try a little of what is "new," have mixed results, and abandon the idea or end up with a soupy blend of the old and new, which really does not meet the mandate for all students to succeed. Instead, students are subjected to an individual professional's "cookbook," which has a few tried-and-true techniques but does not really meet particular students' needs, coordinate curriculum, or make learning meaningful and timeless.

Having lessons that are interesting and fun is not enough; teaching has to matter, and it has to have a design that inspires. Our students understand value and purpose, and we must have a classroom system that builds daily on practices that motivate students *through their own learning*.

INTRODUCTION

This book will share a classroom management and instructional model that can make literacy relevant for all students, better prepare them for college, teach the classics, and make critical thinking an essential component of how one approaches learning. By using this book, middle and high school teachers can easily and confidently change their instructional approach to literacy.

Not only is the book a step-by-step guide, but it serves as a model for theory turned into practice. Every strategy presented is grounded in best practice and explained simply.

Changing one's classroom approach requires confidence and an understanding of why and how this switch informs teaching and improves learning. This guide will provide the support and guidance needed to transition to an instructional model that has demonstrated results in all classroom settings and with every type of learner.

CHAPTER ONE
WHY USE READING AND WRITING WORKSHOP?

Reading and writing workshop is successful because from the first day of school to the last, students are invested in projects that matter to them. Like the literate in our society, they deal with what suits them, and the teacher facilitates their interests. Frank Smith refers to the workshop as a "community of writers" wherein its members share ideas as the teacher, the most learned of the group, monitors the emerging literacy skills of each member. This environment allows for students to pursue topics that make learning important—there is an intrinsic reason for one to think and improve.

Many positives result from this approach: Students work independently, purposefully, and cooperatively; write and read better; and, most notably, develop what Donald Murray refers to as a self-evaluating critical self or the "Other Self," which allows students to apply "thinking about thinking," or metacognition, to tasks. They also develop healthy attitudes about literacy.

Surprisingly, even many honors-level students dislike reading and writing, which is result of a curriculum that teaches at them. (The National Endowment for the Arts reports that the number of "non-reading adults [has] increased by 17 million from 1992 to 2002," while the National Commission on Writing in America's

CHAPTER ONE

Schools and Colleges considers the lack of effective writing instruction in the classroom to be a "writing challenge to the nation.")

Teaching pupils what "they need to know" in a context that they value—their own reading and writing—works exponentially better than having students solve artificial problems or have uninteresting topics about which to read or write. Students are painfully aware of what constitutes school "work" as opposed to what matters to be learned. Much of the apathy that a student exhibits is directly related to schooling that does not make a difference.

Interestingly, psychologist William Glasser posits that schools are not a part of students' "Quality Worlds" because teens do not value what they are being asked to do in the classroom. If we want our students to invest of themselves, we must change the way we ask them to learn.

Many teachers set reading and writing up to fail. They use textbooks with stories that students care not to read and teach writing in a format that they care little to master. It is understood now that purposeful teaching takes place in a workshop class.

CHAPTER TWO
SUSPENDING DISBELIEF

If one is to make the leap to a workshop style, certain myths about teaching have to be discarded, such as students won't work well in groups; they will not read from books on their own or read books that are challenging; they will not write anything of substance and will waste time if allowed to work independently; they will not care about the quality of their work; they will learn nothing from silent reading; creative writing is not real writing; and writing workshop is a remedial or primary grade method of instruction. All of these are false.

Students who are conditioned to be passive and have no say in what they are asked to learn become disenfranchised from the mission of the school, and, while honors students see the grade as a means to an end, those less interested slide further into apathy as the years, for them, drag on.

If one is to persevere in a workshop class, these myths must be ignored, which is no easy task. The reason a workshop model has not been widely adopted is that it is like having a tiger by the tail, and it is comforting to stick to the traditional curriculum: Who wants to be the kook who tries something different or is considered radical? Who wants to try something that she herself is not sure will work? Who will support this initiative to change? Where is the curriculum

CHAPTER TWO

package that comes with this methodology? What if one tries it and it does not work?

There are lots of questions for which there are no easy answers, and, sadly, too many colleagues have told me that they feel like pariahs in their own schools, so why bother?

Rather than deal with each of these concerns, let us imagine the classroom ideal that we first thought possible when we chose to teach; let's imagine a classroom that excites everyone and where learning is empowering. Suspend disbelief for a moment. Hopefully, in the following chapters all these questions, and many others, will be answered.

CHAPTER THREE
FIRST STEP: CHOICE AND OWNERSHIP OF READING AND WRITING

No teaching method will succeed unless students have the opportunity to invest in it. In order to begin a workshop class, a teacher asks students to write creatively and to read books they would like to read. Many students will go out and get books of their own to read in class, and many, with a little help, can begin to write a story or poem. For both, time has to be devoted.

Depending on what works, some teachers set aside two days for silent reading and discussion and two for writing, with another day for other lessons. Nanci Atwell's method from *In the Middle: Writing, Reading, and Learning with Adolescents*, for reading and writing everyday, lends itself to a routine that is easy to manage.

The most common problem that a teacher faces is that secondary students have generally come to dislike reading and writing for any number of reasons but primarily because they have never had the chance to read and write for enjoyment. In the United States, the National Writing Project is built upon the premise that since many teachers are not writers, they struggle to teach it.

In the classroom, not reading and writing for pleasure denies one the awe-inspiring power of creativity, and promoting creativity is the single smartest move a teacher can make. Unfortunately, not all students respond initially. Urban students or students in lower tracks,

CHAPTER THREE

particularly boys, tend to be the hardest to reach. In order to get the workshop class off the ground, a teacher must take certain steps.

Reading

If possible, try to have a small library of high interest, easy read books available either in your classroom or school library (Box 3.1). An energetic librarian who can "book talk" a title or point out books that may interest a student is an invaluable resource. Keep just a few rules for students:

> You have to like the book or else find another.
> You have to seriously try to read it.
> Skimming through the boring parts is okay.
> Writing about your book in your Writer's Notebook (see chapter 4) is a must.

Once all students have selected a book, the teacher logs in the titles and the pages by moving around the room as the class reads. Afterward, the teacher sits and reads. If there are reluctant readers, sitting in the back of the class allows a teacher to monitor reading.

The teacher that reads during "reading time" instead of correcting papers or checking homework gives value to reading and ensures the likelihood that all students will develop the habit of reading. Students who become readers change drastically in terms of behavior and attitude, so it is worth the time and energy expended to set the class up.

Writing

Establish rules for "writing days." Students should be given a folder for their creative work and be assisted with the brainstorming of ideas for writing. Again, reluctant learners need more help. Oftentimes, having them make a list of topics related to anything they

BOX 3.1
High-Interest Classroom Library Titles

Note: Books suitable for high school only are noted with an asterisk (*).

Anonymous: Go Ask Alice*
Armstrong, William: Sounder*
Avi: Wolf Rider, Something Upstairs
Burch, Jennings Michael: They Cage the Animals at Night
Carlson, Natalie Savage: The Family under the Bridge
Chbosky, Stephen: The Perks of Being a Wallflower*
Cormier, Robert: The Chocolate War*
Crutcher, Chris: Running Loose, Chinese Handcuffs*
Fox, Paula: Monkey Island
Gipson, Fred: Old Yeller
Hemingway, Ernest: The Old Man and the Sea*
Hinton, S. E.: The Outsiders, Tex, Rumble Fish
McDaniel, Lurlene: Saving Jessica*
Lamb, Wally: She's Come Undone*
L'Engle, Madeline: A Wrinkle in Time
Lipstye, Robert: The Contender, The Brave
Paulsen, Gary: Tracker, Nightjohn, Hatchet
Pelzer, Dave: A Child Called "It,"* The Lost Boy*
Reaver, Chap: A Little Bit Dead
Sender, Ruth Minsky: The Cage
Sparks, Beatrice: It Happened to Nancy,* Jay's Journal*
Steinbeck, John: The Pearl*
Wagner, Robin: Sarah T.: Portrait of an Alcoholic*
Wartski, Maureen Crane: A Boat to Nowhere.

like, or anything that makes them happy, is a good starting point (see chapter 5).

Once done, students are to be given time to write with no clear ending point for a finished product. Rather, they are to write or show drafts of what they are attempting to write as evidence of a class

CHAPTER THREE

work grade. The best way to get artificial, drab writing or to turn off reluctant writers is to create deadlines. The emphasis should be on writing ideas out completely, regardless of how much class time that might entail.

The teacher then spends time writing when the class does and conferencing with students when it is time to collaborate, and this becomes the day-to-day makeup of the workshop class along with the addition of a Writer's Notebook, focus lessons, and activities that enhance reading and writing.

In the chapters that follow, a number of areas will be discussed in greater detail: the daily routine, grading, how to use the self-selected student work in the classroom, focus lessons on reading and writing, as well as portfolio building. It is important to remember that setting aside the time for students to read and write *for their purposes* is the first crucial step toward creating a successful class.

It is important, too, that the choice and ownership be extended by the teacher to the students, as it has a powerful significance beyond just letting them have a chance to enjoy what they will do: It allows them to build "intellectual capital" in that what they choose to read and write is valuable and worthwhile, which, by extension, indicates that the teacher values their choices and who they are as individuals.

CHAPTER FOUR
THE WRITER'S NOTEBOOK

An invaluable tool for the workshop teacher is the Writer's Notebook (WNB). Over time, it becomes all that a student thinks, learns, and feels about reading, writing, learning, and life. It becomes a daily diary of all that matters to a student, an incredible teaching tool, and it helps sharpen a student's critical and metacognitive thinking. Randy Bomer's book, *A Time for Meaning: Crafting Literate Lives in Middle and High School*, is an excellent introduction to the uses of a WNB.

A regular spiral-bound notebook is all one needs. One half is set aside for private daily journal entries made to begin each class and the other half—the working side—is used for class notes, observations, homework, musings, impressions, brainstorming, and the revision of ideas.

Students are asked at the opening of every class to write quietly about anything at all. The private journal side of the WNB should be respected by others and certainly kept separate from the working side of the WNB. It is an excellent idea for the instructor to model a sample entry on the board or overhead to give the

CHAPTER FOUR

students a sense of what is expected. The teacher's version should be kept simple:

9-5-05
Today is the first day of school. It was hard to get out of bed this a.m. I was spoiled this summer! But I'm glad to be back and start a new year. Many of my students have nice, new school clothes. Lots of the girls are wearing rubber sandals or "flip-flops" and the boys have really sharp-looking sneakers. I wonder what they're thinking about right now. I know I always wondered about my teachers.

An entry like this demystifies writing, in that students usually have a preconceived and a restrictive sense of what they are expected to write when in school.

Students need to write for themselves, not for the teacher. Spelling and grammar are not an issue at this time. All that is needed is the date—clearly labeled at the top of each entry—and that they not skip lines or pages and that they use appropriate language. Although it is not to be read by the teacher, one might overlook an off-color word or two, unless that type of writing becomes too obvious to ignore. By setting up the journal with the dates clearly marked, one can quickly scan the journal portion and assign a grade without reading the entries.

After five minutes of writing every day over the course of a week or so, an expectation of how much to write becomes apparent so that when it is time to review the entries, the teacher can make a quick decision about how consistently a student has attempted to participate.

It is important to stress to students that thinking about what to write is not writing. Students tend to obsess over the form of their response rather than the clear expression of their thoughts. They are to write first, think second. They need to get into the habit of recording thoughts, however random, so that writing at some point becomes as natural, and easy, as thinking.

Why not assign a topic every day for the journal? Because who in the real world is assigned a topic about which to write? Only in school is the topic laid out for the writer; everywhere else the writer is left to her own devices to come up with an idea. Why not train students to do the same? Also, how will students take the initiative to write if they always have to wait for a teacher to assign something for them? Students of every level and ability will fill notebook after notebook without any help, and many times spend well beyond five minutes writing, oftentimes outside of class, without assistance.

As the school year moves along, the WNB becomes the most important "book" they possess; the added benefit is that it is always brought to class. Those who have taught for a while know that having students bring their notebooks with them every day is no small miracle. So don't assign a topic; let them struggle with having to come up with their own ideas. It is the best way to learn to overcome writer's block and fear of the blank page.

Using the Writer's Notebook

Observation Assignment

Besides a daily journal, students need to think like a writer. First, ask them to observe an ordinary activity like a teacher trying to stick a pencil in the ceiling tiles above her head. (Obviously, this is not the type of activity that is normally encouraged.) The idea is not just to record what is done, but to write about it as if it is happening for the first time. Initially, the activity to have them observe is one that begins with the same event so that it can be discussed later.

The class needs to know that the reader should feel like she is experiencing the episode as the class first did in their writing of the event. Afterward, they are to spend time in groups deciding which of their attempts was the best account. The class reconvenes to read and discuss the best versions. The point is to decide which retelling successfully re-creates the moment. The goal is to have students become observers of life and accurate recorders of incidents or situations.

Ultimately, this leads to "showing versus telling" and demonstrates why it is so important for a writer to re-create moments so as to involve the reader. Students come to understand that the power of writing lies in the ability to involve the audience through well-chosen words, and it is also a good way to discuss point of view since they have to write the event in the present tense.

Having students do observation assignments of moments that matter to them creates an excellent foundation in the WNB for future stories and a reflective place for thinking and discussing writing. Also, it allows for the consideration of the proper use of verbs, detail, and word choice, which are easier to explain in this context rather than in a grammar or literature text.

Allow students to write and observe other events—like gym class or someone sitting in the library—for two weeks or so and then ask them to read through their entries, notice any similarities or oddities, and assess whether or not their writing is improving. They reflect on their observations, of course, as another entry.

Finally, ask them to rewrite one entry to share with a group to see what type of improvement they are making. Each group will peer-edit with the notion that the revised piece must create a picture in their minds or make them sense that they are witnessing the event. A sample peer-edit sheet would like this:

Writer: _____ Date: _____

Title: _____

Critical Group Member (peer editor): _____

Directions: Listen to the work presented carefully and answer the questions that follow. After hearing the *first written observation*, answer the following in your WNB. Remember that you will share this response with your classmates.

First Observation

What was your reaction to the observation? What did you like or remember? Could you picture the event in your mind? Did any of the details provided appeal to your senses? What would you suggest to make the moment more real?

Revision of Observation

Before the written observation is read to you, ask the author what to listen for—the writer generally has a good idea of where the possible weaknesses are—then listen carefully as it is read to you and answer the following questions: What was the improvement and why did it make the writing stronger? Did the revision of the piece fit what you had in mind for it? If so, why? If not, what would you suggest? Did you notice anything here that might apply to your writing?

This assignment can take a week of class time that is well spent. Out of this comes a focus lesson such as, "Why is this sentence well written?" Just putting a strong student sentence on the board can illuminate the power of active voice or vivid detail better than any grammar exercise ever could because the lesson is grounded in an activity that matters to the students as writers. Not only will important teaching points surface, but this activity reinforces a number of thinking, listening, and reading strategies.

Students are asked to create mental pictures; they compare their writing to the writing of others; they rethink and revise their work (Box 4.1); and they are in the ongoing process of trying to write like authors would, thus developing an appreciation for the craft and, ultimately, creating an expectation of how a book should read.

Students learn how books should engage them as readers, which is an important strategy. Students can spend many years studying fiction but never develop an expectation of how to think about a work until they attempt to write. When attempting to write fiction, they must learn the craft of it, which gives students an idea about how an author connects to her audience.

Looking for the author's design or craft for storytelling is an excellent strategy to help them take apart a text. Asking questions such as, "How do you feel about the main character?" "What do you think the real problem in this story is?" "Is there something in the story that the protagonist should know about another character?" can give them a way to look at how characters are developed, how details are added meaningfully, how sentences move ideas smoothly, how key moments in a story come to life, and what, ultimately, the author is trying to do for—or to—the reader.

Also, it can give them a confident, critical stance by which to take apart the writing of a professional.

In Robert Probst's "reader response" methodology, he argues that readers can build thinking about text based on their emotional reactions to the elements of a story.

Writing about Reading

By the second month, writing about reading begins in the WNB. Students continue to do observations as homework, but after every self-directed reading session, they write about their books as well.

They write about anything that springs to mind as they read or what they remember when they are done. Usually, no more than five minutes is required, and after two weeks, students in reading groups book talk based on their notes. At this time there is no need to use a peer-edit sheet or guidelines, just let them discuss what they have read and listen for similarities in titles or themes.

Sometimes, a list of prompts for writing about the books will help them focus on theme, plot, or comprehension (Box 4.2), but most of the time they like to write about what they have read and what came to mind. Often, the teacher points out that the types of books they have read are not unlike the types of stories that they have written in

> **BOX 4.1**
> **Observation Assignment**
>
> *Directions*: Write all your answers in complete sentences and on white lined paper. This activity is worth five As.
>
> (1) Search through your Writer's Notebook. Find three observations with a connecting theme. Write the theme and why you think it occurred more than once in your notebook.
>
> (2) Again, search through your observation notebook. Pick out what you feel is your best observation. Answer the following questions based on that observation:
>
> - Does it have a lot of detail explaining the event or object?
> - Did you report it as it was happening?
> - Did you provide your reader with a description that would create a picture for him or her? How did you do this?
> - Name five descriptive words used in your observation.
> - Why do you consider this your best observation?
> - What can you do to improve it?
>
> Use your ideas about how to improve your observation to rewrite it. Pass in the original and the new version.

class. Surprisingly, many are not aware of the connection. Also, students tend to read similar books, and that can lead to a genre study or evaluation of a single author's works written in the form of longer papers that are argumentative, persuasive, or theme based.

Students spend the rest of the year writing about reading for a few reasons: The retelling aids comprehension, discussion can center on why some books were better than others, and students find who likes to read what type of book and why—a critical discovery when attempting to build a literate community.

Many points raised in class about a novel, from how it opens and ends to everything in between, are evaluated critically from the

CHAPTER FOUR

> **BOX 4.2**
> **Writer's Notebook Reading Prompts**
>
> - Did you pick the book because of the cover art? What do you expect the story to be about?
> - You are the main character. Write about what has happened to you during today's reading.
> - What keeps you interested in the book? What keeps you reading?
> - Imagine that you are in the story. What character would you like to speak to or change?
> - Are all the characters real? Why or why not? (If you're reading a true story, the author still has to include details and dialogue that makes a character realistic.)
> - After what you've read today, what do you think will happen in the next few chapters or scenes?
> - Did anything in the story surprise, anger, sadden, or please you?
> - Were there times when you were confused with the story?
> - Are you finding the words or writer's style hard to read? Which words or sentences are they?
> - Did what you read remind you of anything in real life?
> - What seems to be the most important idea in the book?
> - Can you imagine acting as the main character might?
> - Do you want to learn anything as you read this book?
> - What major decision, choice, or action does the main character face?
> - Is there a character in the book you don't like?
> - Describe the place where the main character was (pick one if necessary). Do you notice anything about the place, and does it help you understand the story better?
> - If you could be any character in the story, who would you be?
> - Did anything you read today remind you of a similar situation in your life?
> - How would you design a cover for the story?
> - Were you happy with the way the book ended?
> - What was the most important issue in the book and how was it resolved?
> - Is there a movie or song like this story?
> - In your mind, what does the main character look like?

standpoint of author's craft and style. Students talk about what matters to them, which is critical to their understanding and enjoyment of fiction and, ultimately, helps them progress through the stages of reading development.

The WNB grounds reading and writing in a context that is meaningful to students. This methodology is based in reader response theory and the emotional reaction that a reader experiences in relation to a text. An emotional reaction provides a mental avenue for thinking about a story meaningfully. Intimate, spontaneous feedback to text from peer to peer or student to teacher allows for discussions in pupil-friendly language.

The Reading and Writing Link

When working with a WNB, it is important to constantly link the reading of stories with the writing of them, and not only through student work but through that of professional authors, too. Generally a comment such as, "This book is stupid!" is annoying, but this comment can be expanded with, "What don't you like about it?" Expect to get an answer such as, "The character doesn't act right," or "The story is boring." These responses occur when reading and writing are linked. In the next chapter, we will see that the establishing of a writer's workshop that facilitates discussion about reading is as important as the writing itself.

Note also that not all writing in the notebook has to be educational: Students should have the opportunity to respond to the artistic intention of the work. Randy Bomer reminds us that not all poetry and fiction need to have a teaching purpose.

Sometimes instructors need to ask pupils to listen, read, and think about how a work affects them. The aesthetic response is to be valued and considered: What is the effect of this work on our minds and hearts? What do we feel? Hear? See? Think about as we read or listen to the piece? These questions free our students from the idea that reading always has to have a purpose—that it has to be figured out in order to be understood—and can help them relax as writers as well.

CHAPTER FIVE
THE WRITING WORKSHOP

To be clear, the work of Donald Murray, *A Writer Teaches Writing*, and Nanci Atwell, *In the Middle: Reading, Writing, and Learning with Adolescents*, is the foundation of a workshop approach, which borrows heavily on their ideas and organizational strategies. Essentially, without their scholarship and practice, one might never have the opportunity to be reinvented as a teacher of literacy.

Donald Murray coined the phrase "writing process," which unfortunately has been codified by textbook companies into an artificial process that, sadly, does an immeasurable injustice to the insightful and practical teaching strategy that his work conveys.

The writing process is a thinking and planning strategy that is adaptable to any writer, regardless of one's proficiency, yet each year it is taught as a system, which stifles the beauty of it and harms the development of young writers. In fact, the writing process is generally taught in such an elemental way—a possible writing idea in the center of the paper and the bubble map of thoughts that relate to it—that it actually harms many students at the secondary level who are ready to write—all they need is time.

Teaching the writing process as this "one way" to begin actually dumbs it down, creating unnecessary steps that bore writers or make it seem like this is how to plan to write, and that is the greatest injustice to the process.

Donald Murray talks about writing as critical thinking and a way to activate one's "Other Self," the voice in our heads for which we write, the voice that challenges us to do our best work. How one activates and ultimately utilizes the Other Self is the goal, and whatever path a student may take to begin writing is unique to the student. Teachers need to work with those who need help getting started and get out of the way of others who can go off with an idea of their own.

Writing workshop begins then by having students write—and not the five-paragraph dinosaur, "What I Did on Summer Vacation," but with a poem, rap, fantasy, novel, short story, song, or whatever else they fancy. Just as we let students choose what to read, they will be allowed to choose what they write. (A note of caution: Temper the teacher self that wonders: *What's being learned here? How is writing a creative piece about a dog that ran away improving grammar? They need to learn nouns and verbs!*)

And what of the teenager who refuses to write or just stares at a blank piece of paper all class? The first step is to get the class focused on writing and then deal a bit later with the reluctant writers.

Assuming the majority of students are willing to begin, start with student-generated lists of favorite items like movies, places to go, places they would rather be, most interesting events in their lives, people they admire, what they do in their spare time, friends from childhood, favorite vacations—obviously, these categories can go on and on.

The idea is to get them thinking about what matters to them. Students should circle the items that are most interesting or thought provoking and free write about them for ten minutes in their Writer's Notebooks (WNBs).

After a time, they should have some material with which to work, and by using the board or overhead the teacher can help them to see the story potential in their free writing by offering it to the class for suggestion or comment.

CHAPTER FIVE

Using just the first sentence or two of a student sample allows the class to add interesting elements or prompts them to expand the idea into other story possibilities. Are there elements of mystery, drama, action, or suspense lurking in the sample?

If a student were to offer a short recollection of a first-grade field trip to the zoo, for example, many story possibilities could be explored. What if the teacher running the trip left the author at the zoo at the end of the day? What if the school bus crashed or an animal escaped? What if a fire broke out? Again, possibilities can grow from whatever the free write involved.

For students who aren't reluctant to write, it takes little prodding to get them going. They are probably good readers who have active imaginations and can build a story or poem out of a few short writing opportunities. It is also a good activity to take an opening sentence and expand it for the class.

"I left her alone." This brief sentence is an example upon which a story can be built. Who left her alone? Why? Where was she? Who was she? How old? Listing the many responses of the students on the board helps explain how a writer thinks about an idea and how that idea can blossom into a story.

At this point there are two concerns. First, avoid giving students something to write about either in terms of topic or physical item. Writing about how an orange rolls around on the teacher's desk is not meaningful—it is artificial—and just a writing exercise that is viewed as just "practice."

To extend the analogy, athletes will tell you how they live for games and generally practice with less enthusiasm. The same holds true for writing. If it is seen as practice writing, then it will be stilted and uninspiring, but if it is generated from one's imagination, then the game is effectively "on" and the likelihood is that it will be intensely written and thoughtfully attempted.

The second concern is appropriateness of topic. Students are reminded as they begin to expand a topic that it must be suitable for class. In other words, graphically violent stories or those with vulgar language are not acceptable. There is a way to write about a date rape that gets the message across without being so detailed as to be titillating. Also, there is a way to show that a character is tough without having to resort to profanities.

It is good to tell students that the novels they may hopefully publish in the future can be as realistic and profane as is necessary, but in a classroom the sensibilities of others should be considered. What is appropriate for school should not be that hard to fathom or adhere to during the day.

Another great way to begin writing is to take them out of the room and let them observe an outdoor gym class, nearby elementary schoolyard, a street area, or any busy place and ask them to write as much as they can about what they see in as much detail as possible, in a way similar to the early observation assignments. Again, taking a few of these and putting them up on the overhead screen for the class to see is a great way to talk about what is in them or what is missing.

Sharing ideas and thoughts about writing in this way opens the eyes of all to what others think and write; it helps students compare themselves to others, allows them to be more comfortable, and takes the first steps toward creating a writing community.

Reluctant writers, on the other hand, pose real problems when beginning, and boys tend to be reluctant and sometimes downright obstinate when it comes to writing. Girls tend to take to writing, which supports the research that girls are generally ahead of boys in literacy development.

Most boys will not write because they have suffered at the hand of the red pen, and the emphasis on correcting writing for spelling and grammar has left them feeling "dumb and stupid" in their words. These reluctant males are often poor readers too, which adds to their dislike and disinterest in Language Arts. Also, there may be a social dynamic in that it is not "cool" to write—which is just a way to look tough rather than dumb in front of friends—or it may be that writing is not culturally acceptable.

CHAPTER FIVE

A Hispanic teenager once refused a teacher's prompts to write because if he did, he would no longer be the dominant male in the room. In cases like these, it is best not to push the issue but let it resolve itself.

The students who feel inadequate will come to see that they can write the same types of stories as the others. Through the sharing of ideas and drafts, they become more comfortable and eventually make an attempt to write. They are encouraged by the fact that the class drafts and that these first, poorly written attempts are not corrected but just listened to and commented on, which proves to be a relief to those traumatized in the past by the red ink.

Of course, there will be some who do not write for a long time, and once their interests are known, it is sometimes easier to give them an opening sentence to work with like "I fumbled on the goal line" or "It followed me home." These are first sentences that can spark a student's imagination, particularly if one likes football or would like to write about a stray dog.

Once the reluctant writer begins, it is important to let her know, as it is for all the others too, that writing is a process of fits and starts and that the best ideas can fizzle out. Actually, this is an excellent lesson about how writers and writing works—or does not—from time to time.

Many issues related to writing a longer work can arise: Story ideas tend to appear in spurts and just because one plot line reaches a dead end, it does not mean the ideas were not worthwhile; students tend to lose interest or become hypercritical when the inspiration fades, but there was a reason the idea sparked their interest and it is worth rethinking it; sometimes the initial draft goes so far afield that the original idea was lost, so revision becomes an essential skill.

It is also important that students learn the value of their thoughts, and they are never to throw out an idea. Beginning writers are notorious paper crushers, balling up paper after paper in frustration. Whatever they write, even if they feel it has no immediate value, they are to keep it because words are links to ideas, and those thoughts may later fall into place one day like stepping-stones. And students need to know that this is how one thinks: Ideas are clues to a larger puzzle.

Managing the Reading/Writing Workshop Class

Once they are writing, there is a need on the teacher's part to write with them. Always begin with a daily, fifteen-minute quiet writing time where the instructor can model writing while sitting in the middle, side, or back of the room—never in the front—and keeping a writing folder of her own.

Modeling writing, or any literacy activity, can never be overemphasized. If it is important enough for the teacher to insist upon, then it must be important and worth doing. Sitting in the class, and not in the front at the teacher's desk, creates a sense of shared activity, which builds a sense of community that encourages all to write.

In a writing workshop class students need quiet time to write, share writing with others, revise, conference with peers (and later with a teacher), and produce final drafts that best represent their original ideas.

Nanci Atwell's book, *In the Middle: Writing, Reading, and Learning with Adolescents*, well documents the writing of each student, but it can be modified to suit one's approach. Over time, the teacher finds a best-fit way to monitor students, who are essentially working independently on pieces of various genres and length.

An example of a monitoring strategy is the "Two Pages, Twice a Week" (Box 5.1) rules adapted here from Atwell; these rules keep students writing and meeting the expectations for class productivity.

The first rule is that the students are free to write about what they want, as long as it is appropriate. The second rule is to begin on yellow paper and just write without regard for spelling, grammar, sloppiness, or cross outs. Colored paper helps track who is in what stages of the writing process. The only demand is that students not throw anything away, and if they want to start a new idea, they can

CHAPTER FIVE

> **BOX 5.1**
> **Writing Workshop—Two Pages, Twice a Week**
>
> 1. You are free to write about anything you want! Always start writing on yellow-lined paper—this will be your *first draft*.
> 2. When you finish what you've written, you must read it to two or three others. They are to fill out a *Listener's Checklist* for you, which you will turn in later.
> 3. Rewrite your first draft *neatly* on white-lined paper—this will be your *second draft*. (Please write on only one side of white paper.) Staple a *Writer's Checklist* to your second draft and have it checked again by at least two others in the class. When you get it back, make the corrections suggested by your peer editors. (Editors check for grammar, spelling, and whether or not your writing makes sense to them.)
> 4. Staple the corrected second draft, Listener's Checklist, and Writer's Checklist together. I will read what you've written and return it to you. Again, you will have to make corrections so that you can have a correct, *final copy*. Final copies are to be saved for a portfolio.
> 5. It is important that you *ask permission* before you do anything! Also, you will be graded by how well you cooperate, behave, and finish what you start. All writing is to become final copies.
> 6. Remember two things: Be polite when you talk to someone about what they've written, and you're never done—you can always start a new writing project.
> 7. Grades are either A, F, or 0 for class work, behavior, class materials, or assigned work—no excuses, no exceptions!
> 8. Don't bother someone if they're busy—ask me for help.
> 9. Please stay in your seat until called up to my desk.
> 10. It is important to observe the quiet writing time of the class.

THE WRITING WORKSHOP

brainstorm lists or details right below where they abandoned the first pieces. What matters is that after two class periods they have a sheet of paper that has writing—however choppy or messy—written on both sides.

At this point the pupils have earned their first class work grade, an A for effort (more on A, F, or 0 grading in chapter 6). If a student has yet to finish "two pages"—one sheet written on both sides—then she has homework.

Every two days, the teacher is to move around the room with a grade book and put the date on the pages that each student presents for a class work grade. Putting the date on each page allows for the tracking of the progress of a piece, since some can get quite long and so one can also keep track of the "kings of the first drafts," those students who never go beyond the drafting stages to complete a finished item.

Following through with a set of drafts allows one to monitor the progression of a writer's growth and measure skill acquisition, so moving the first-draft kings along is vital to instruction. Also, pieces that grow too long in a first-draft format need to be broken up into chapters so that the editing process does not overwhelm the peer editors in the room.

Usually four pages of a first draft need to then be read to two classmates who complete a Listener's Checklist (Box 5.2). The checklist reinforces the elements of a story or poem; asks listeners to focus on pacing, logic, and word choice; and also provides positive feedback from one's peers.

The third rule is to then take the first draft and rewrite it neatly on white-lined paper so that it can again be peer-edited for spelling and grammar (Box 5.3). This step is the most difficult to build with the students and requires many important whole-class focus lessons to help make peer-editing and proofreading work effectively.

Teachers often say this stage of the process is the key weakness in workshop methodology in that students do not peer-edit well, and, as a result, teachers still end up with quite a bit of correcting to

CHAPTER FIVE

BOX 5.2
Listener's Checklist

Listener's name: _____ Date: _____

Title: _____ Written by: _____

(If needed, use back of sheet to complete your answers. If this sheet is not used for a story, answer the questions that apply. *This is a class work grade.*)

1. Who or what is the main character (protagonist)? _____
   _____

2. What does main character look like? _____
   _____

3. Where does the story take place? (This is the setting of a story.)
   _____

4. What words do you remember and why?_____
   _____

5. What words show action? List four of them. (Words like played, ran, smiling, and so on are called verbs and they tell us what a noun is doing. A noun is a person, place, or thing.) _____
   _____

6. Can you list six descriptive words like tall and blue (these two words are adjectives because they tell us about nouns) or quickly and now (quickly or now are adverbs because they usually tell us about verbs)? _____
   _____

7. What types of problems do the characters have? (These problems are known as conflicts.) _____
   _____

THE WRITING WORKSHOP

8. How are these problems solved? (This is called the resolution.)
   _____

9. Is it a mystery, horror, romance, suspense, comedy, adventure, or drama? More than one? Explain. _____
   _____

10. Does the opening sentence get your attention? _____

11. Do scenes follow along and make sense or would you make any changes? Explain. _____
   _____

12. What do you think the writer wanted you to understand from reading this piece? (This is called a theme.) _____
   _____

13. Did the characters act realistically? If not, explain. _____
   _____

14. Did all of the words or sentences sound right to you? If not, explain. _____
   _____

15. Did this writing remind you of something else you may have read or something you might know something about? _____
   _____
   _____

Remember that you must answer these questions after the story is read to you! If you can't answer all the questions, then *listen to the story again!*

CHAPTER FIVE

do. They argue that giving students time to peer-edit is time wasted, but peer-editing is part of the process of learning grammar and good writing habits, so it is an important step.

What has to be understood about peer-editing is that students have never been primarily responsible for the correcting of their work, the teacher has, and that is the first change that has to take place. If not, they move from year to year without a sense of how to read a written piece for errors—or strengths—and thus they become dependent on others.

In life, no one reads a paper for them, certainly not the superior who hired them in the first place, so to expect our students not to develop a strategy to proofread their work is a major failing of instruction—but that's what instructors do when they don't invest the time in building critical self-awareness.

To begin creating what Donald Murray calls the "Other Self," the voice in our heads that makes us self-critical, teachers need to stick to the essentials of grammar and mechanics and use "user-friendly grammar." For example, verbs have quite a few tenses, but does it matter that one knows the past perfect tense? Maybe for a quiz bowl competition, but not for the beginning writer. All a writer needs to know is that verbs are to be consistent in terms of tense or "time" (as referred to on the Writer's Checklist) and that they need to be active, not passive.

When revising or rereading, it is much easier to look for words like "was" or "is" in a paragraph for verb consistency than it is to wonder about the past perfect tense.

Keeping grammar simple helps move writers along and makes peer-editing work. The entire Writer's Checklist is designed to make the evaluating of one's piece—or that of another—easy and focused. As a result, the expectation is that students will pick up on the errors of others, and, if not, then they should be at the teacher's desk explaining why.

Evaluating the work of others is a class work grade, and unless a student has real grammar or spelling difficulties, a teacher should ex-

BOX 5.3
Writing/Peer-Edit Checklist

Paper written by: _____ Date: _____

Please check all papers for the following items. *Use a pencil* to mark corrections on the writer's page. *Circle the number of any item on this paper that you think is or may be incorrect.* Remember, this is a class work grade.

Edited by: _____ and _____

1. Sentences begin with capital letters; capital letters are not mixed with lower case, and all sentences end with a period or proper end mark.
2. The following words are not confused: to/two/too; they're/their/there; are/our; hear/here; right/write.
3. Writer wrote on line and wrote neatly.
4. A lot, all right, and all other words checked for proper spelling.
5. Commas are used to separate more than one adjective.
6. Abbreviations like "+" or "w/" are not used.
7. Only one of the following words is used in a sentence: and, but, or, so.
8. "Time" in a paragraph is the same. (For example, is/was; run/ran are not used in same paragraph.)
9. New paragraphs start when writer changes speaker, place, time, or idea.
10. Active voice, such as "He pushed the boy," is used instead of passive voice, such as "The boy was being pushed."
11. "Got" not used at all!
12. Corrected words that the writer didn't know how to spell.
13. Pronouns "match" nouns they replace: A student should study; he (*not they*) needs to be prepared for college.
14. Verbs are alive. Instead of "walk" use wandered, sauntered, or skipped.

(continues)

> **BOX 5.3 (continued)**
>
> *Correcting keys:* Use these symbols for errors found on the page you edit.
>
> Indent/new paragraph: np →
>
> Mixing capitals, misspelling, or word misused: Circle word and write *SP* over it for spelling error.
>
> Follow margin/write on line/don't write to edge of page: Lightly draw straight lines an inch from each side of page to show how words are out of place.
>
> Overuse of "and": Cross out "and" then insert period in its place.
>
> *Note:* Editing is an important part of your grade in this class and it helps you learn many grammar and spelling rules. Be sure to do the best you can. *This sheet is to be handed in with any second draft.*

pect to see improvement over time. What the teacher learns by using peer-editing is that there are those students who have an affinity for when to start a new paragraph, how to check for spelling, and so on, and it is a good idea to ask them to sit with a classmate who may be struggling and let the paragraph "expert" run the conference.

Pairing up those who can with those who can't insures mastery of skill for the expert, provides individual attention to the student who needs it, and takes the correcting burden off of the teacher, whose job it is to *facilitate* writing—an idea with which instructors tend to have trouble because they are so used to dominating the class agenda.

By leading focus lessons on common grammar and writing errors during the early stages of writing workshop, one sets up expectations for grammar, spelling, and mechanics before the second draft phase. Writers are then expected to read their work closely, which improves their work in general. The grammar checklist provides for some easy focus lessons and simplifies the basics.

Editing, Conferencing, and Generating Final Copies

How one responds to student work is critical to the momentum of the workshop class. Pupils who are encouraged to revise and have the opportunity to get positive, constructive feedback from teachers and peers grow exponentially as writers, learn to avoid mistakes, and understand how to write from strength.

Following the rules of "writing day," a revised second draft with a Listener's Checklist and Writer's Checklist is turned in to be final edited. (At this point, any major errors should send the instructor to review the checklists to determine if any concepts need to be taught again to the class.) Using a pencil, the teacher line-edits the work like a proofreader would, even adding corrections as needed. It is important to point out the positive aspects of the piece as well, usually by writing notes in the margin.

With the return of the work, a student also receives a "skills sheet" (Atwell) with these headings above three empty columns:

Title of Work	Skills I Learned	Skills to Learn

This sheet becomes a running record for each written piece submitted of what was done correctly and what needs to be done better. Noting teacher and student conferences and what was discussed in specific detail, helps the student.

Too often comments in the Skills to Learn column are vague such as, "words confused," which should read, "they're = they are; there = place; their = belongs to them—don't confuse." Remarks like these help students remember what they did wrong, especially when they see the skills sheet in front of them in their folders, and it allows them to present work to the teacher that over time needs less and less editing.

When line-editing, a pencil is better because almost all writing is intensely personal and a self-conscious endeavor: A red pen speaks to correctness and eradication of error; it does not speak to the writer and her growth. It is the thinking associated with a piece that has to be developed fully, so an overemphasis on correction and the errors one makes—which the red pen heralds to everyone—is counterproductive.

A pencil-edit is less intimidating and allows for the building of meaningful dialogue between teacher and student, and this dialogue is at the heart of developing good writers.

In fact, one builds trust with reluctant students by being more aware of how they feel about their work and abilities, which opens the door to real learning. Those who argue for a red pen when editing have never made the effort to truly write and take the risk of sharing their work with others (or have forgotten the associated anxiety). Only those who have invested heavily in writing and the sharing of it know how important it is to be respectful and sensitive to the efforts of others and would never think of using a red pen.

Another important point about editing is that one should comment on a paper as if they were reading it for the first time. When making margin notes, ask questions about a character's motivation, for example, that can lead to discussion during a conference and give the writer an idea to expand. While a student waits for the teacher to discuss a paper, the author can be thinking about what was written in it and that too can add to the meaningfulness of the dialogue about her work.

The conference itself should take no longer than five to ten minutes—it is not the time to go into great detail about every error or comment on the paper. When dealing with many serious errors, the best method is to have a short conference on the first two pages or so, have the student redo the page, and conference again later on what is left.

It is never a good idea to explain too many concepts at one time. Rather, one needs to walk a student with many difficulties through the process step-by-step so as not to discourage or overwhelm. Eventually she will complete an assignment that, now done correctly, can serve as a benchmark for other pieces. The student now has an example of her own work as a model, and this allows the teacher to use it to raise expectations of what the student is capable of doing.

During the conference, it is important to see if a student is aware of the errors made by asking questions about grammar basics.

Many times errors are the result of carelessness, so it is good to ask first. It is also a good time to ask questions that expand the student's understanding about the craft of storytelling. Many students write plot-heavy stories: a sequence of events for which the reader knows little more than A was followed by B, which was followed by "The End." The conference is a good time to expand on all the elements that make for great writing; you may not ever get that necessarily, but it is crucial to open the writer's eyes to the craft of storytelling so that they become effective readers of the works of others, including published authors.

As a writer becomes more aware of the elements that make a story interesting for the reader, they also develop a writer's eye for effectiveness in the novels that they read, and this is a critical thinking strategy that cannot be overstated. Good writers, as Frank Smith (1998) notes, "read like writers," in that they look for what they like in the work of others that they can then incorporate into their own pieces.

Lastly, never forget to talk about what is good in a student's piece.

It is not enough to say that a section is "good"; rather, what, specifically, is good? Is there variety in sentence structure? Is there voice? Are the characters real? These are the types of comments that need to be discussed and explained. Getting an A on a paper without knowing specifically why is worthless. How can one get an A on the next paper if one only has a passing understanding of what was done right the first time?

Conferences should give all students a specific sense of what is strong, weak, or potentially wonderful. If not, one needs to think how to handle conferences so that there is an equal mix of correction and promise, and conferences need not be scheduled like little appointments.

CHAPTER FIVE

Conferencing can be as informal and casual as a conversation that takes place in the hall before class or during a walk around the room. By quickly reading the first few paragraphs of a student's work each day, one can find something to say about a piece that shows interest or helps move the idea along. Talking about writing is essentially the commerce of the class, and one needs to be alert to every opportunity to do so.

Once a paper has been evaluated and reviewed, the student then produces a final copy that becomes part of the working portfolio. At midsemester, students will then begin the process of selecting pieces that will go into a year-ending summative portfolio.

Building upon an idea from initial draft to final copy is the day-to-day activity of the workshop class, and it is as unique an activity as the students in the class: Some work on long projects, others short, but in all cases, they are working on something that matters to them. Being invested in their pieces creates an opportunity for the instructor to teach students what is essential to the effective telling of their stories and not just skills related to artificially generated topics, which are then only done to produce a grade.

Standing back to observe the class, one sees time devoted to quiet writing, peer-editing, conferencing, and revision. Students are working either cooperatively in pairs or alone, depending upon need, and are also at different stages of the writing process, which requires a teacher who moves around the room to check on pupils and to step in as necessary.

In the workshop class, many key teaching and learning concepts are being taught: reading and writing fluency, grammar, spelling, mechanics, story basics, listening and editing skills, revision, and the habits that make writers confident, creative, self-motivated, and successful. Students also learn—through conferencing with an instructor and a peer—about how they think and, ultimately, that problem solving is not linear but a series of starts and stops that lead to a solution.

Academic Writing

Once the workshop model is in place, it is time to add the overlay of formal writing to the work of the class. The early days of the school year are used to lay the groundwork for a reading-and-writing class that focuses on fluency, but toward the end of the first quarter, it is time to teach the class about the types of writing expected in an academic or professional environment.

No matter what the class or level, it is always good to establish how to respond to an essay prompt by rephrasing the question as part of the opening sentence, introducing the reader to the topic to be considered, explaining what the main point of the essay will be (thesis), and then, in the body of the essay, taking each point and finding expert evidence or text references to support each contention. Finally, the essay ends with the summation of the evidence and how it supports or argues for the thesis.

In some cases with reluctant writers start with the basic essay format (Box 5.4), using a handout that goes into the writing folder. (It is best to laminate it into a poster that can hang in the classroom as well.)

With less-skilled writers or younger students, walk them through each aspect of the basic essay format. A short excerpt from a novel like the one from *Go Ask Alice* in (Box 5.5) works well.

Pupils begin by responding to the excerpt in their WNBs, then sharing the entries to others in small groups, and, finally, listing similar thoughts about the passage on the board or overhead until they come to some consensus of what could be written in response to the prompt. Since they have now formed opinions, the students must now consider how it was that they came to these conclusions.

Students are asked to highlight or underline sentences or words that helped them develop their ideas about the excerpt: These are the "facts" or text references they will use in the body of

CHAPTER FIVE

> **BOX 5.4**
> **Basic Essay Format (Outline)**
>
> Use this outline to write an answer for an essay question.
>
> In the first paragraph:
> Always begin by rewriting the question as part of the first sentence of your essay. If the question is—Can you find an important idea in this passage from Go Ask Alice?—please write, "An important idea from this passage in Go Ask Alice is . . ." and give your opinion to complete the sentence. (Your opinion is also called a *thesis statement*.) To finish the paragraph, add another sentence or two to explain how you know this or why you feel this is the important idea.
>
> In the second paragraph:
> Use an actual example from the passage to support your opinion. For example, on page 78 she writes, "I feel like an adult." Then explain why this example supports your opinion: Alice feels like she's treated as a child at Christmas until she finally has the chance to help the adults clean up after Christmas Day. Helping out makes her feel grown-up.
>
> In the third paragraph:
> Sum up your answer by rewriting part of the question and your opinion as you did in the first paragraph. Please write: Alice finally has the chance to help the adults and this makes her feel grown-up. Feeling like an adult is an important idea in this passage from Go Ask Alice.
>
> *Note*: How many paragraphs would you need if the question asked for two, three, or six examples of important ideas?

their essays to support their opinions. A step-by-step drafting process is built, beginning with the introduction that rephrases the question—necessary to insure that students write and respond directly to the prompt—and includes the newly formed opinion about the excerpt. (Notice again the reliance on Robert Probst's

> **BOX 5.5**
> **Author's Theme**
>
> Theme: *The author's reason for writing a story or poem. The theme explains what the author values or believes is true about life.*
>
> Directions: Read the excerpt from *Go Ask Alice* by Anonymous and answer the essay question using the basic essay format.
>
> Essay Question: Can you find a theme in this passage? Be sure to cite the words of the author to support your opinion. This assignment is worth 5 As.
>
> Key to understanding the excerpt: Consider how she feels in this diary entry.
>
> > December 26
> > The day after Christmas is usually a let down, but this year I enjoyed helping Mother and Gran clean up and put away and take out. I feel grown-up. I am no longer in the category with the children, I am one of the adults and I love it! They have accepted me as an individual, as a personality, as an entity. I belong! I am important! I am somebody!
> > Adolescents have a very rocky insecure time. Grown-ups treat them like children and yet expect them to act like adults. They give them orders like little animals, then expect them to react like mature, and always rational, self-assured persons of legal stature. It is a difficult, lost, vacillating time. Perhaps I have passed over the worst part. I certainly hope so, because I surely would not have either the strength or the fortitude to get through that number again.

reader response method: The students initial, emotional reactions are recorded in the WNBs, shared with peers and the class, and eventually become the basis for written essays.)

Again, depending upon the type of student, one class period is used for reading, responding and brainstorming, and then another

CHAPTER FIVE

period is for drafting a three- or four-paragraph essay. In some cases with reluctant students, it has to actually be done sentence by sentence.

The purpose of this exercise is to give the students a template to use in the future. It is not to create scripted writing, although that is what is happening at first. One reason why writing fails is that students have no real plan or design for their essays, despite being taught outlining, paragraphing, note-taking, and note cards. (It is time to finally deep-six the three-by-fives. Who doesn't have a dime to make a copy of a page on the library's copy machine?)

Providing students with a template and posting the exemplary essays that result from using it create benchmarks of expectation for academic writing that also make conferencing about pieces easier.

The basic essay format is the basis for academic writing, and from the basic essay format all other expository writing is built, including the research paper, and no matter what students eventually write, one should take a minute to show them how it is an expansion of the basic format. Pupils cannot write effectively in any format without this blueprint in mind: Introduce the reader to your topic and provide your opinion, next find text references to support your ideas, and, finally, use this evidence to convincingly sum up your argument.

Notice that not a lot of teaching time is spent on transition sentences, explaining what a thesis is or where it should be, hooking the reader, or clinching the idea. While these are all good concepts, they are all that ever seems to be taught about essay writing, and too often this terminology and insistence on detail (for example, where the thesis statement *must* be placed) keeps students from seeing the larger picture, doesn't help them think effectively about how to use their initial thoughts as the foundation to build their essays, and generally distracts them from clearly presenting their ideas.

Not that transition sentences are not important, but what do nonwriters have to transition to?

Generally, what makes a student's essay great is the natural sound and use of language, a logical thesis, a concise conclusion, and facts that support the writer's argument, but this cannot be solely taught as a blackboard lesson. Great writing simply arrives from time to time in the flow of a workshop class, and when it does, using it as a lesson for others makes it timely and fits nicely into a learning context—unlike a lesson done at the board.

Obviously, what's learned in the context of trying to write is better than a lesson taught *before* trying.

A beautifully worded paragraph written by Martin Luther King in "Letter from a Birmingham Jail" will bring shrugs of recognition from students, but it will not make that type of writing attainable in their minds.

On the other hand, a nicely worded transition sentence by a classmate makes growth as a writer tangible and within reach. Having a sense of what is best about their writing, and sharing it, is how the terminology of grammar, mechanics, style, and voice become relevant to the work of the writing community.

Once the basic essay format is understood, the next step is to ask students to write a critical work, either a book summary (Box 5.6) or a book evaluation (Box 5.7) about a silent reading selection. Each has a template and a sample of student work to use as a model, which makes students aware of how the basic essay format is used in all essay writing, so much so that it becomes a part of how they plan to write. Part of the midterm and final exams asks students to respond to written prompts without the reliance on a visible template, so the understanding of academic form eventually becomes committed to memory.

The better students become with the form of an essay, the better they are able to focus on voice, creativity, and originality in their prose.

During the school year, depending on the ability of the students, they might be required to write two book summaries and complete a book evaluation essay by midterm and then another evaluation and a compare-and-contrast essay (Box 5.8) to round out the year-end portfolio. More capable students will begin with a book evaluation and move through a compare-and-contrast, Book Link (Box 5.9) or Author's Theme project (Box 5.10) to a research paper.

CHAPTER FIVE

> **BOX 5.6**
> **Book Summary Essay and Outline**
>
> Follow this outline when writing a summary of the book you've read. A summary is a *brief* retelling of the important parts and ideas of the story. Begin at the top of the page with the following:
>
> Title: (List the title of the book and underline it. Always underline the title of a book.)
>
> Author:
>
> Date: (List the date you're writing this summary.)
>
> Skip a line and begin your summary.
>   In the first paragraph, tell me what the entire book was about within five to eight sentences—no more. Begin with (for example): The book, <u>Treasure Island</u>, was about a boy named Jim Hawkins who sails on a ship—then describe the rest of the story. After you finish this paragraph, *don't skip a line, indent from the margin,* and begin the next one.
>   In the second paragraph, tell me if you liked the book or not and why—this is your opinion or thesis. (Don't tell me that you liked some parts and disliked others. *You either liked the book or not; make a decision.*) You could begin with this sentence: I didn't like the book because the characters didn't seem real to me. One to three sentences to explain why you didn't like the book will be enough.
>   In the third paragraph, you need two examples from the book to support your opinion. You could write: On page 170, Jim cries because he's all alone, and then take the actual words out of the book and put quotes around them. "I sat in the barrel and cried." This part didn't make sense to me. He should have been happy to be alive.
>   After you find another example and explain why it supports your opinion, you need an ending sentence. You should rewrite your opinion like this: These examples show why I did not like <u>Treasure Island</u> because Jim Hawkins did not seem like a real boy. Remember,

> whenever you take words exactly from a book, you need to put quotation marks around them—*if you are unsure on how to do this see me.*
> The summary will look like this:
>
> Title: <u>Go Ask Alice</u>
> Author: Anonymous
> Date: October 26, 2006
>
> <u>Go Ask Alice</u> was about as teenage girl who is hooked on drugs. This book is a diary of her experiences. She writes about her life, her struggle to stay off drugs, and the pressure she faces as a teenager.
> I liked the book. I thought it was realistic, and I could understand the problems she faced.
> I liked the parts when she writes about how hard it is for her to stay clean because her friends put a lot of pressure on her to go back to her old ways. On page ** she writes, "_____." This made me realize how her old friends would do anything to make her do drugs. Later on page **, I was sad for her because her friends threaten her saying, "_____." This was unfair. She was trying to stay off drugs but they wouldn't let her. These are the reasons why I liked this book. I could understand the problems she faced.
>
> In all, the entire summary should be a page in length. Write the summary on white-lined paper and hand it in to me when finished. I expect you to look over your summary to make sure there are as few errors as possible. *This assignment is worth five As.*

Usually with those of lesser abilities, two of every essay type is required to be sure that pupils have mastered the easier version before tackling the more difficult one in the continuum.

When using these essay outlines, keep those student essays that are exceptionally done and staple them to the essay outline sheets as a model to follow. Once the student gets the outline and a student essay to review, the process of writing each essay moves smoothly and provides a basis for conferencing and revising.

CHAPTER FIVE

BOX 5.7
Book Evaluation/Outline

Directions: Use the following outline to write an evaluation of the book you have read.

First paragraph: Give your opinion of the book in terms of whether or not it meets the standards for a well-written book—this is the thesis of your paper. *You must mention the three standards for a well-written book that you have selected from the list that apply to your book.*

Second paragraph: Summarize the book in four to six sentences, just like you would at the beginning of a book summary.

Third paragraph: Write about one of the standards you have selected, quote an example from the book that supports the standard then *explain* how the quote fits the standard. *This is where most writers make a mistake because they do not explain why the quoted passage supports the standard.*

Fourth paragraph: Write about the second standard you've selected; quote from the book to support it, then explain how the quote fits the standard.

Fifth paragraph: Write about the third standard you've selected; quote from the book to support it, then explain how the quote fits the standard.

Last paragraph: Rewrite your opening first paragraph here and refer to your opinion.

Note: Before starting your evaluation essay, you are to decide if the book is well-written or not by looking over the standards list. Use your overall feeling for the book (whether you like it or not) to help shape your opinion. Then go to the standards list and pick three reasons from the list to support your opinion of the book. The standards are on the back of this sheet. Pick three that apply to your book then start your essay.

STANDARDS TO EVALUATE
A BOOK OR SHORT STORY

From William Appel and Denise Sterr's *The Truth about Fiction (Writing)*

Standards are generally accepted rules for determining the quality of a written work.

- The first sentence is interesting and puts the reader right into the middle of the thoughts or actions of the main character.
- The story is told through the eyes of no more than two main characters. (This allows the book to have a consistent point of view, which adds dramatic tension to the plot. In other words, as the story moves along, the reader grows more concerned about what will happen to these characters.)
- The characters are made real by how they talk and act.
- The setting of the story fits the characters and action of the story. (Horror stories have dark, gloomy, scary places for their characters.)
- The theme of the story fits the actions and thoughts of the main character. (Theme is the main idea behind the author's writing of a story. You could think of it as a moral, but it's not—a moral is told to us at the end of a story while the theme is suggested to us by the way the characters act and live their lives.)
- The story is always moving forward. One scene leads naturally to another.
- The author lets the characters tell the story by letting us see how they react to other characters or events.

Note: You are to pick three of these for your book evaluation essay and write them into your essay to support your opinion. It might be a good idea to do a first draft of your essay, then show it to someone before turning it in for a grade. This essay is worth six As and is the main assignment for your reading this quarter.

Note: Include a bibliography for the books in your essay. For example,

(continues)

CHAPTER FIVE

> **BOX 5.7 (continued)**
>
> **BIBLIOGRAPHY**
>
> (Listed by author's last name in alphabetical order.)
>
> 1. Burch, Jennings M. <u>They Cage the Animals at Night</u>. Albany, NY: Avon Press, 1992.
>
> 2. Sender, Ruth M. <u>To Life</u>. New York: Bantam Books, 1988.
>
> (This information is found on the first page of the book, not the first page of the story.)

Advantages of Benchmarks and Templates

Regardless of whether one teaches in an inner-city school or not, the national mandate is the same: All students are to learn and this learning is to be demonstrated on individual state testing.

The mandate makes clear that students are to meet higher, tougher standards—no excuses; if they do not the school district and its teachers, no matter how hard they have tried, are failures. Encouraging support, isn't it?

One should not expect much from an educational bureaucracy that perpetuates the long-revered myth that states can test their way to better schools. Can testing help? Sure, it is a way to take a snapshot of a district, but expecting student performance to improve based upon it is limited thinking at best.

In any event, success on state testing is the classroom teacher's burden to bear, which is why benchmarks and templates work so well: They allow a teacher to move quickly and effectively in reading and writing and actually plan for where students' demonstrated reading and writing growth and performance should be at any stage in the school year. They also establish quality of work, classroom

BOX 5.8
Steps to Begin a Compare-and-Contrast Essay

This is an essay where you compare—and find the differences between—two or more subjects. For this assignment, think of two books you've read that you could compare and contrast. Pick two items from the "Standards to Evaluate a Book" list (*at bottom*) that apply to both books. Decide which novel is the better written because of the standards you've selected, then follow the outline below.

ESSAY OUTLINE

First Paragraph: Name the two books and which one you think is the better written one, then mention the two standards of a well-written book that you'll use to support your opinion.

Second paragraph: Summarize the plot of one book.

Third paragraph: Summarize the plot of the other book.

Fourth paragraph: Write about how one book meets standards you've selected; give an example from the book (mention page numbers and quote scenes) to support those standards and explain how the quote supports the standard. This is to be done for all quotes used to support the standard.

Fifth paragraph: Write about how the other book doesn't meet the standards you have selected, quoting pages and scenes from the book to support your opinion.

Sixth paragraph: End your essay by saying that these are the reasons why you feel that (*title of book*) is a better written novel than (*title of book*) because it meets the standards you selected (which are? repeat them).

Note: This assignment is worth twelve As.

(*continues*)

CHAPTER FIVE

> **BOX 5.8 *(continued)***
>
> **BOOK STANDARDS**
>
> - The first sentence is interesting and puts the reader right into the middle of the thoughts or actions of the main character.
> - The story is told through the eyes of no more than two main characters. (This allows the book to have a consistent point of view, which adds dramatic tension to the plot. In other words, as the story moves along, the reader grows more concerned about what will happen to these characters.)
> - The characters are made real by how they talk and act.
> - The setting of the story fits the characters and action of the story. (Horror stories have dark, gloomy, scary places for their characters.)
> - The theme of the story fits the actions and thoughts of the main character. (The theme is the main idea behind the author's writing of a story. You could think of it as a moral, but it's not—a moral is told to us at the end of a story—the theme is suggested to us by the way the characters act and live their lives.)
> - The story is always moving forward. One scene leads naturally to another.
> - The author lets the characters tell the story by letting us see how they react to other characters or events.

expectations, and help a transfer student get onboard quickly without a lot of explanation.

From the description of a workshop class, one can see that it has a momentum that builds upon prior work, and by the second month of a year, students are well into the routine and ongoing projects of the class. As work is completed, it is posted in the room for others to read and, most importantly, refer to when needed.

Think of where a class like this leaves a transfer student: So much is happening independently, how will she ever be acclimated? How can she catch up? Since the workshop class has built-in protocols,

BOX 5.9
Book Link Project

The purpose of this essay is to link at least three of the books you've read with at least two of the following: theme, main character, genre (book type: mystery, horror, nonfiction, romance, adventure, drama, suspense, comedy), or your interest in them.

PLANNING YOUR ESSAY

1. Decide which of the three books by the same author to write about.
2. Decide how you will link them. For example, you might link them by mystery and main character, or you could use theme and your interest in them. Make sure you understand this step—ask me if you are unsure.
3. Plan your essay. Review how book evaluation and compare-and-contrast essays are laid out. The Book Link Essay will follow along like they do—with some differences—because you're writing about more than one or two books.

PARAGRAPH OUTLINE

Directions:

1. Decide what each paragraph will be about and provide a sentence to explain what you will do with each paragraph.

    For example, in the introductory (first) paragraph, you might write this:

    > In this paragraph I will describe the three books I've chosen and how I will link them.

    (Note: "Introductory" means to introduce the reader to what it is you are going to write about and what they will read.)
2. Look at book evaluation and compare-and-contrast essays for ideas. (Hint: Talk about each book separately).

(continues)

CHAPTER FIVE

> **BOX 5.9 (*continued*)**
>
> 3. Explain links to each book.
> 4. Provide one example from each book to show link. (Remember, there are three books here from which to show examples—remember the "paragraph" math!)
> 5. Conclusion.
>
> ### PARAGRAPH OUTLINE WORKSHEET
>
> *Directions:*
>
> Use the lines below to list what you will add in each paragraph. Turn this worksheet in for review before you write your essay. (Note: My "okay" on this worksheet does not mean your essay will be perfect.)
>
> This worksheet counts as five As toward a total of twenty (20) upon the completion of this assignment.
>
> Name: _____ Date: _____
>
> The first draft of essay will be turned in on: _____ (Take an educated guess but remember I like work turned in when? Yesterday!)
>
> ### PARAGRAPHS
>
> 1. Introductory.
>
>   _____
>
>   _____
>
> 2. Summarize all three books.
>
>   _____
>
>   _____

> 3. Discuss first link with one example from each book.
>
> 4. Discuss second link with one example from each book.
>
> 5. Discuss third link with one example from each book.
>
> 6. Conclusion.

it becomes a matter of determining how fast that student might acclimate based, primarily, on attitude and on skill.

When a new pupil arrives in class, determine whether this student seems interested in Language Arts. Does she read or write? What were her prior classes like? What does she remember from those days? This information is gathered as part of a first-day activity that's done with all students. Having students on the first day describe their literacy creates a sense of how to proceed.

Any number of questions can be asked to help a teacher better understand a student's mind and heart regarding Language Arts, learning, and school.

If a student seems receptive to reading and writing, then acclimating to the class requires little more than an explanation of the rules that manage the workshop and the chance to sit with a student in class to get situated. Because the routine becomes second nature,

CHAPTER FIVE

BOX 5.10
Author's Theme Project

Directions: In this essay you will look at three books by the same author that you feel have the same message, idea, or theme. You are to find an example from each one and, along with a discussion of their endings, argue that the books have a similar theme or main idea for the reader.

1. *First Paragraph*: Introduce reader to the topic. What is the author's theme? What is the reason for writing the book? *The way to find the theme is to think about the problems the main characters had and how they were solved.* From the result of these solved conflicts, the reader can get an idea or message about life from the author. What do you think the author wants you to learn? In this paragraph state your thesis (opinion).
2. *Second Paragraph*: Summarize plot of first book.
3. *Third Paragraph*: Summarize plot of second book.
4. *Fourth Paragraph*: Summarize plot of third book.
5. *Fifth Paragraph*: In this paragraph, write about the last book summarized (third book). What is the main idea, message, or theme? Give an example from the book and explain how this example supports your opinion. Mention how the book ends. Does it fit what you expected might happen? Does the ending support your idea of the theme?
6. *Sixth Paragraph*: Do the same with the second book as you did for the last book in paragraph 5.
7. *Seventh Paragraph*: Do the same with the first book as you did in the last two paragraphs.
8. *Eighth Paragraph*: Based on your examples from the books and your discussion of their endings, write a conclusion that summarizes your opinion (thesis).

Note: This assignment is worth twelve As. See attached essay for help. Include a bibliography.

former students can come into the class and help work with groups of new students on the first day of school, so integrating a new student at any time is not difficult.

Students who are reluctant learners require a slower pace not unlike that taken in the beginning of the school year. What helps is that the assignments missed, and the resulting quality responses for them, are posted in the room. The new student can get plenty of guidance from looking independently at them. So without explaining much, a new pupil can get up to speed with not only what was missed, but how assignments are to be done as well.

Another advantage of templates and benchmarks is that they maximize conference time. It is very easy to refer to the assignment's requirements when it, along with a proper response, is set before a student as a comparison. Pointing out where the student's paper went awry makes it easy to talk about format and the necessary revision.

Not surprisingly, those who write poorly have a very difficult time following the template. They often lack the concentration needed to follow through with the piece, or they let undisciplined writing habits overwhelm any sense of structure and organization, so bringing them back to the expected format is a great way to train them. And the discussions with students are about the actual written piece as opposed to a rubric, which many times only confuses the issue and doesn't give writers a concrete understanding of what needs to be improved and why.

Rubrics, by and large, are of little use to a student unless they are written in specific terms and come with examples. Most rubrics are written for teachers in that they identify and codify acceptable grade level products, but they do little to help writers. A rubric that reads, "Ideas are clearly expressed," means nothing to someone who has no reference to which to compare, so how is she to judge?

Finally, the benefit of templates and benchmarks is that they empower students to move at their own pace.

A capable pupil will work through the assignments without much teacher input, which then frees the instructor to spend more

CHAPTER FIVE

time in conferences with others. Providing a template and then posting exemplary responses moves the class quickly through many types of writing exercises, gives them a sense of expectation, helps them with revision, and encourages them to work independently and confidently while freeing up the teacher to work with others. As a result, precious class time is maximized.

Another way to establish expectation for what will be taught and learned is by using a Personal Literacy Goals sheet (Box 5.12) or a Language Arts Assessment Checklist (Box 5.11) adapted from Shayne Trubisz's template. The assessment sheet is something that is used with middle school students, freshmen, or reluctant learners. The checklist establishes what they will be expected to know and helps me plan where they are as individuals and as a group.

The Personal Literacy Goals sheet has four basic categories. The learning outcomes are generated by brainstorming the goals to which they should aspire in order to be more proficient in each category. The goals are then added to a list that is kept in their writing folders. Focus on three thinking domains—cognitive (skill building), affective (how students respond and become engaged in learning), and metacognitive (thinking about thinking)—and lead them toward class goals.

All three areas are critical in terms of reading and writing basics, self-motivation (affective), and critical awareness and revision.

As the year progresses, students are asked to find work that reflects the acquiring of the skills listed and then explain how it does. This is actually a critical analysis and persuasive writing activity that is directly related to their work, to which they respond well because it gives them some control over their learning and allows them to see real progress. Establishing goals early in the year also helps them get a sense of the long view of the class and the purpose of classroom lessons.

In the first few weeks, then, they are actually talking about how all the work they will do will result in the learned skills and abilities

BOX 5.11
Language Arts Personal Assessment

Name: _____

As a reader I
- Always keep a book with me to read .... Yes/Not yet
- Read without interruption .... Yes/Not yet
- Identify main characters .... Yes/Not yet
- Visualize the setting of a story .... Yes/Not yet
- Recognize the tension [conflict(s)] in the plot ... Yes/Not yet
- Know which character is telling the story (point of view) .... Yes/Not yet
- Identify metaphor and symbol .... Yes/Not yet
- Determine the author's purpose (theme) .... Yes/Not yet
- Read through slow parts or parts I don't understand .... Yes/Not yet
- Recommend a book to someone .... Yes/Not yet
- Imagine scenes and dialogue in my mind .... Yes/Not yet
- Figure out words I don't understand .... Yes/Not yet

As a writer I
- Sit quietly and write .... Yes/Not yet
- Brainstorm for ideas .... Yes/Not yet
- Keep a Writer's Notebook .... Yes/Not yet
- Try writing a poem .... Yes/Not yet
- Revise drafts until paper is written as well as possible .... Yes/Not yet
- Use end marks, commas, and quotations properly .... Yes/Not yet
- Use active voice rather than passive voice ...... Yes/Not yet
- Use variety in the way I build sentences .... Yes/Not yet
- Self-edit my work and the work of my classmates .... Yes/Not yet
- Correctly rewrite all papers returned to me ..... Yes/Not yet

(continues)

BOX 5.11 (continued)

Use pencil to edit the papers of others	Yes/Not yet
Try to learn from those who are strong writers	Yes/Not yet
Use a thesaurus to add new words to my work	Yes/Not yet
Write at least twice a day in a Writer's Notebook	Yes/Not yet
Put the proper headings on a letter/envelope	Yes/Not yet
Use "see," "saw," or "had seen" correctly	Yes/Not yet
Keep "time" the same in a paragraph	Yes/Not yet
Correct run-on sentences or sentence fragments	Yes/Not yet
Make sure all writing ends up as a final, perfect copy	Yes/Not yet
Keep handwriting as neat as possible	Yes/Not yet
Use capital letters for proper nouns	Yes/Not yet
"Show, don't tell" when writing a story or poem	Yes/Not yet
Think about my audience before I write	Yes/Not yet
Know what type of written format is expected by the reader	Yes/Not yet
Plan my response to include facts to support my opinion	Yes/Not yet
Know my strengths and weaknesses as a writer	Yes/Not yet
Write persuasive, critical, argumentative, or compare-and-contrast essays	Yes/Not yet

As a learner I can

Follow rules for reading and writing days	Yes/Not yet
Not disturb others as they work	Yes/Not yet
Follow directions as well as I can	Yes/Not yet
Expect to make mistakes and correct them	Yes/Not yet
Listen carefully to others and speak as clearly as I can	Yes/Not yet

THE WRITING WORKSHOP

> Be patient and raise my hand when I need help .... Yes/Not yet
> Avoid making the same mistakes over and over ... Yes/Not yet
> Bring everything I need for class with me
>   every day .... Yes/Not yet
> Share my work with others .... Yes/Not yet
> Not make fun of the writing of my classmates ... Yes/Not yet
> Be cooperative and polite .... Yes/Not yet
> Respect the privacy of others .... Yes/Not yet
> Always have something to do .... Yes/Not yet
> Finish work ahead of time for extra credit ...... Yes/Not yet
> Remember to use what is taught to me .... Yes/Not yet
> Think about why my work is either correct
>   or not .... Yes/Not yet
> Use school as a time to improve as a student .... Yes/Not yet
> Have goals for myself and stick to them .... Yes/Not yet
> Be on time and prepared for every class .... Yes/Not yet
> Get help when I need it .... Yes/Not yet
> Never wait until the last minute to
>   do something .... Yes/Not yet
> Focus on the good things I can do .... Yes/Not yet
> Be confident that I can improve upon
>   my weaknesses .... Yes/Not yet
> Think about how I learn .... Yes/Not yet

discussed during the first week of school, so there is no wonder as to where the schoolwork undertaken will lead.

These early expectations shape the year and bring the end in sight right from the beginning. The course has a purpose and design visible to all, including parents, which is another bonus. Parents have a real sense of what the teacher is trying to do and why, which is very helpful when dealing with difficult, unmotivated, or unfocused students.

Parents, too, worry when a teacher seems to be "different," so establishing expectations that can be charted and monitored to show

BOX 5.12
Personal Literacy Goals

During the school year, I will focus on these goals.

READING AND WRITING FLUENCY

- I have a positive attitude about reading and writing.
- I am willing to read and write on my own.
- I know reading and writing helps me think and use my imagination.
- I will read and write until it becomes easy to do.
- I will read and write every day.
- I make connections from the books I read to other books, my life, and to the world.
- I will use my Writer's Notebook to record my thoughts, feelings, class notes, and observations about life.

CRITICAL SELF-AWARENESS

- I understand that learning about reading and writing is an ongoing process.
- I learn from my mistakes.
- I have a sense of what I do right and on what I can improve.
- I expect that reading and writing will be difficult sometimes, and I will use strategies to work through those moments.
- How I read and write reflects who I am as a reader, writer, learner, and thinker.
- I know when I need the help of others.
- I am always aware of those who can help me.
- I will try to write and read about topics that I know are challenging to me.
- I reread and rethink as I read and write.
- I am aware of my audience and what is appropriate.

CRITICAL AWARENESS OF OTHERS

- I know I can learn from others.
- I always reflect upon the comments of others.
- I practice applying what's suggested to me as to how I read, write, learn, and think.
- I know the value of positive and constructive comments.
- I know that being negative has no value.
- I know that others can get help from me.
- I know that my behavior and attitude does have a positive influence on others.

AWARENESS OF ACADEMIC EXPECTATIONS

- I know that I need to be on time, prepared, mature, and thoughtful.
- I know to turn in the best work of which I am capable.
- I know that I am expected to ask for help.
- I need to be aware of what will allow me to be successful in class.
- I can read like a writer.
- I can see the world like a writer.
- I will draft and plan before I write and include facts to support my opinion.
- I know that a variety of sentences, use of active voice, and "showing not telling" make fiction stronger because these better involve and entertain the reader.
- I know what I do well when I write, and I know what type of errors I am likely to make.
- I know how to write essays that convince, compare, analyze, argue, and entertain.
- I know to turn in neatly written papers.
- I use a dictionary, thesaurus, or grammar book when needed.

real literacy growth is essential. Deviating from the normal, traditional curriculum is not easy; one encounters doubt from all directions, especially from teachers in one's own school, and it can be a high-wire act in some respects, so the better sense one has of best practice in literacy and integrates it into a week-to-week plan that meets the needs of all students, the more confident one becomes as each day passes.

A criticism often heard about templates is that it leads to scripted writing that drowns out student voice. The romantic, traditionalist viewpoint would certainly agree, but the teacher pragmatist screams loudly and clearly that until students begin to like to write, understand the format needed to deliver their ideas effectively, and know how to polish their prose, voice is buried under a multitude of errors and writing disinterest, which is the norm for a high school class.

Even students with a facility for language need to understand form and expected response so that they can maximize their ability. Experience shows that almost all students need templates and benchmarks if their writing voice is to be discovered.

CHAPTER SIX
GRADING

When B. F. Skinner, the behavioral psychologist, taught at Harvard, he used an A, F, or 0 scale, which has often been incorporated into a workshop class. This grading scheme motivates students to revise, sets meaningful class expectations, establishes real-world values for the quality of work produced, and simplifies grading. It works by establishing that all writing will reach a level of proficiency and, until it does, it needs to be revised.

For example, if the activity is to write a business letter, then an A grade would be earned when the letter produced is as one would expect a business letter to be: clearly written, logical, and in the proper format with no obvious errors. This type of expectation encourages dialogue and interaction between students and the teacher because no paper can be improved upon without input from the teacher and peers through conferencing, revision, and review of model letters.

A grading system that tells students that they will work on these until they are up to standard can initially be frustrating for them, but in the long run they will learn to make their writing stronger and to avoid the obvious writing errors and mistakes that are specific to their work.

CHAPTER SIX

Another advantage to this type of grading is that it is non-negotiable: It is either up to standard or not, unlike most grading methods. For example, when using a typical rubric that has numbered levels and subcategories, a student gets an average score for a written piece. Asking those students who are satisfied with an averaged grade of three on a five-point scale to revise can be frustrating, particularly when the student chooses to ignore a score of one in a field. As a result, a key aspect of writing is not redone because the pupil is more focused on the grade and not on the quality of the assignment.

With an A, F, or 0 scale, the entire paper has to be revised or the writer takes a less-than-passing grade for the assignment. The F essentially notes that the student attempted the task and thus earns a grade for effort, but does not earn a passing grade since the quality of the work is less than what is expected. In almost every case, students come to see the value in revising.

First, they can earn their grade if they make the effort; second, they get direct help with the revisions and develop a sense of how to avoid the types of errors they, specifically, are prone to make. Overall, writing becomes easier and they gain confidence. Box 6.1 is Barry Lane's discussion of the B. F. Skinner model from Lane's book, *After the End: Teaching and Learning Creative Revision*. The excerpt is included because of Lane's eloquent argument for a process that is learning—not grade—oriented.

The Skinner grading scale fits every aspect of the class including exams and final portfolios (Box 6.2). Adopting the Skinner model and then adapting it to the entire workshop class makes grading simple and focuses students on reading and writing better than any rubric ever designed. Many students like the idea of earning an A for the course. Having the opportunity to earn a grade creates a work ethic since grading is now about quality and is effort based. The aspect of earning a grade puts all students on equal footing.

The overall grading practice is to encourage students to produce high-quality work, understand the value of revision, be respectful of

BOX 6.1
What about Grades?

When B. F. Skinner taught at Harvard, he gave As and incompletes. Everything else, he surmised, was negative reinforcement and would not help his students to learn. There is not one major study that proves that grading helps anyone to learn. There have been hundreds that have proven it is detrimental. Yet educators, administrators, and school board members continue to insist that students be graded, and, as long as they do, teachers must devise their own strategies to devalue grades.

Here are some simple suggestions to decrease the negative qualities of grades in your classroom.

- Never grade an individual paper. Rather, grade a student's overall progress as seen in a portfolio, specifying areas of improvement. If you grade a body of work, you will give students a better picture of their overall strengths and weaknesses.
- Discuss the negative qualities of grades with students and be very clear about your desire to have them write for themselves and their audience, not for a grade. (Note: There is an irony here, because only this will get them a higher grade. Reality, unfortunately, isn't always ideal.)
- Create criteria with your students and let them evaluate and grade one another's work in pairs. Ask them to compare their grades for each of the criterion. If they differ by more than one point in their scoring, ask a third student to mediate or do it yourself. The goal here is to find a commonality of language.
- Give students a grade for risk. Even though this might be a subjective category and differ with each student, without giving it credence there is no way to legitimize its reality. To reward risk with a grade is in some ways the ultimate contradiction because grades encourage the opposite.

(continues)

CHAPTER SIX

> **BOX 6.1 (*continued*)**
>
> For a writing teacher who believes in encouraging revision, graded papers are nothing less than a curse. Low grades discourage and high grades imply that a piece is done. Even worse, students begin writing to improve their grade instead of finding out what they have to say. In reference to the perils of successful publication, Robert Penn Warren said, "Ambition is the death of the poet." Grades, like success, promote ambition, not education. They create and foster a codependent relationship between student and teacher that revolves around the central question "What do you want?" instead of "Why am I here? What can I learn? What do I have to say?" or even "What can you teach me?" As students wean themselves from external motivators like grades and as they become empowered to assess their own progress, they begin to understand that learning is much more than receiving praise or enduring punishment; learning is an ongoing personal process that can be both frustrating and fulfilling; learning is its own reward.

others, be properly prepared for class, manage class time wisely, work well independently, and always be busy.

Many times one is frustrated by the underachiever who is placed in the class not because of her skill level, but because of her lack of work ethic or poor behavior. This student can pass tests with minimal effort and numerically pass the class without contributing anything to it and, in many cases, may be a disruptive or negative influence to boot.

Moving from a rubric- and test-oriented grading scheme to one that rewards effort (Skinner's model) puts those who would just sit back and underachieve on shaky ground; they have to produce or their grade suffers dramatically.

The message here is that effort-based grading is the norm for the class, especially for those students who did have to work hard to earn a grade. Now effort is valued, the lack of it is discouraged, and not trying is not rewarded.

BOX 6.2
Grade Scale for Academic Writing, Class Work, and Extra Credit

A++ (100) Assignment meets the class criteria for a properly done assignment. No errors in spelling, grammar, or essay format are present. The assignment is written as neatly as possible; has factual evidence from a primary source (novel, text excerpt, short story, poem, film, video, newsprint) to support opinion; is thoughtful, detailed, imaginative, or creative; displays an attempt to be as well done—and thoroughly done—as possible; and is done correctly on the first attempt. Great care by writer to create an exceptional response is obvious.

A+ (95) Same as above; no obvious errors exist in paper's presentation (grammar spelling, neatness), format, or response (no lack of primary source evidence). A minor error or two may be evident, but overall the paper is well done on first attempt. Answers may not be as well thought out or as thorough as in A++ response.

A (90) Same as above; a few minor errors may be present, but paper is well written and meets the criteria for a properly done assignment. Response may also have been a revision of a paper that received a lower grade. *This grade is the expected result of all written work in the class. Any paper failing to meet this grade must be revised.*

F (60) Obvious errors requiring a rewrite exist. *Revision to an A grade is required.*

0 No reasonable attempt was ever made to complete the assignment.

(continues)

CHAPTER SIX

> ### BOX 6.2 *(continued)*
>
> ### CLASS WORK GRADES
>
> Students are expected to bring materials to class, follow class routine, complete work in a reasonable amount of time, not distract others, be well behaved, and keep busy with assignments, revisions, or extra credit work. After a warning, a grade of F is entered in grade book if misbehavior continues. Any subsequent warnings for same incident will change the F to a zero (0) and parents will be notified.
>
> ### EXTRA CREDIT GRADES
>
> Students have the opportunity to earn as much extra credit as possible. Extra credit can oftentimes offset an F received for class work, and opportunities for extra credit are explained in a letter to parents and explained to the class during the first week of the semester.

Finally, all valued activities in the class are graded the same way: reading silently, working in one's Writer's Notebook, completing the writing folder, adding to portfolios, peer-editing, conferencing, revising, drafting, behaving properly, working in class, doing homework exams, writing research papers, and engaging in any other classroom assignments. Some assignments, though, are weighed differently as they would under any grading system, but the earning of the A is still consistently applied. So when checking on students, Atwell's status of the class grading list is kept, which is, essentially, a copy of the class roster page from the grade book.

As the teacher visits with each pupil, a grade for her effort for the day would be an A, F, or 0, depending on what was attempted. Students who were not working are easy to spot and warn. Any student who does earn a 0 can go home and make up the work for an F grade the following day. (It many not seem like much, but an F is scored as a 60, so it is worth doing.) My grades were recorded as A++ (100), A+ (95), A (90), F (60), 0. A typical week in a grade book for a pupil might look like this:

Reading / A, A, A, A, A = 90
Writing / A, —, A, —, A = 90 (Writing is checked every other day.)
Class work / A, F, A, A, A = 84

Aside from the easy math ([90 + 90 + 84] ÷ 3 = 88), a pattern of the student's overall productivity emerges, which makes monitoring easy. Doing a status of the class involves only a quick check of students as they sit and work, but it is invaluable for having a sense of where each student is in a workshop-style class. Also, every day matters and is reflected in the students' grades.

Finally, any type of traditional assignment, test, quiz, or homework assignment can be changed to an A, F, or 0 grade. An exam could be in four parts, each part graded separately. Even a twenty-question quiz could be graded as needing 16 out of 20 to earn an A. (Mathematically, it would be an 80, but 15 out of 20 is a 60 grade on the A, F, 0 scale, so it does need to be a bit forgiving.)

What's left to do is determine what assignments should count more in the grade book, not unlike what is done for a chapter test as opposed to a spot quiz. The grades listed above were all weighed equally, but an essay assignment could be worth five times as much, and the math would be factored in the same as the chapter-test grade would be if it were worth five times more. For example, a grade line for a student might look like this:

A, A, A, A, A, [F (5)] = (90 × 5) + (60 × 5) = 450 + 300 = 750 ÷ 10 = 75

Again, adapting the Skinner grading model is not unlike using a regular scale, and some teachers opt to record the actual numerical grades instead.

CHAPTER SEVEN
BRINGING LITERATURE INTO THE CLASSROOM

Once, during a professional-day activity to revise the English curriculum for the district, a participant said rather matter-of-factly that while all this effort was well meaning, the bottom-line result was that "the textbook is the curriculum," and he was—and continues to be—right.

The chosen textbook series in a school district is the be-all and end-all of literature instruction. The notes about authors are given, the stories are barely read or understood, the class "discusses" what the story "means," and then it is on to another one—or maybe a novel is assigned to break up the boredom.

The two words in the last sentence are quoted because the discussion is generally the teacher doing all the talking; what the story means is what the teacher's guide decides it means, and the great literature, designed to create a whole host of feelings and thoughts and intent revealing something meaningful about the human condition, dies in the classroom. Worse, the passion to be creative and thoughtful that this great writing should inspire has the opposite effect, and many educated adults eventually stop—and in some cases even despise—reading and writing.

And this is what happens on a daily basis when we let the textbook be the curriculum.

Sitting in on a British or American literature class, one feels as if it were a history course. The only reading and writing is the taking of notes from an overhead projector on the culture and time in which the author lived.

(I filled in once for a teacher who had left four pages of handwritten notes on overhead transparencies about Poe's "The Fall of the House of Usher." When we reached the one that explained what the cracks in the walls "meant," I stopped. Dismayed, I asked the students if this was how the class always went. Instantly, a student raised her hand and my hopes rose. She said, "Oh, no. We usually have at least six pages of notes.")

The problem here is that while the intent is good, the result is debilitating, since it is the context for the presenting of literature that is wrong. Relying on the textbook anthology is a great way to make English majors or experts out of the students, assuming, of course, that the students want to major in English, but not all students do.

If we are going to bring literature meaningfully into the classroom, we have to teach reading and writing in a context that allows our students to appreciate what the great authors have done and can teach us. Otherwise, the authors and their works just become notes on an overhead projector with no resounding or lasting melody, and that is the ultimate shame of it all.

Creating Context for Literature

Until one attempts to write, literature can only be appreciated from afar, like the way one looks at paintings on a gallery wall: Some are admired, and even with a basic sense of art, few are understood. What is truly known about the author's vision, craft, or intended impact? Often when preparing a short story for class, teachers rely heavily on the teacher's guide, which is always locked in a cabinet before leaving school at the end of the day. Without the guide, one has little to say or teach, and one is vulnerable to an intelligent remark or question. Without the teacher's guide, one is not a teacher, but once the writing process becomes a part of the class, that changes.

As we grow as writers, we begin to look at fiction for what it can tell us about the craft of creating an effect on a reader. How does one write about love? Or create characters that matter? Or keep the reader interested from the first sentence on? By midquarter the question wasn't "What should I write about?" but "How do I write better about that?" We look to find writing that helps inform our writer selves.

When considering what fiction to introduce, no longer think that American or British literature or the stories in any other text need to be taught in chronological or thematic order as presented by the textbook publisher. Rather, look at any and all available fiction and poetry for what it could do to help the class with what is being worked on at the moment. Do, though, teach each class with an overriding focal point, depending on the course and level.

American literature can be taught with the idea that one studies these works for what the authors tell us about our culture. Early in the school year spend a few days—after the reading/writing workshop is up and running—writing about and then discussing the following questions: What does it mean to be an American? Who are we and what do we believe in? These questions will lead to quite a bit of debate on topics that range from politics to current media to school organization. The idea is to eventually prepare them to answer the question: How does the work of the authors we will read define America and being American? (This question, they know, is to be part of their final exam.) Reading from Poe to Hemingway, they will jot each author's thoughts on culture, politics, and life in general in their Writer's Notebooks (WNBs) and at different times, usually after they work through a packet of condensed readings, list those ideas.

In time, a growing sense of how our famous authors' views reflect and influence our culture emerges.

Considering that the readings from Poe, Emerson, Thoreau, and others are difficult—and keeping in mind that difficult text can stop

BRINGING LITERATURE INTO THE CLASSROOM

the process of reading fluency in which so much time is invested through self-selected student reading—design packets that students can read on their own. These author units focus on just what can be learned from a literary work without having to explain it to the students. In order for the students to work independently, put in margin notes, change a few words, or summarize sentences so the students can get the sense of the language of the work as well as the ideas.

Often one is given easy versions of *The Odyssey* and *Romeo and Juliet* to use with low-functioning classes. Unfortunately, these are so removed from the original language and voice of the author that there is no point in using them. The idea for teaching these texts is to give pupils the basic understanding of the story, but to what end? Reading and writing does not improve, and one can summarize the story or play in a fraction of the time.

Instead, try pulling key scenes out of the originals, setting up the scene with a brief summary, giving them an original version that has the margin notes and simplified words in critical places, and letting them tackle the text (Box 7.1). Once they realize that they can read through these, the value in linking them to their writing is evident.

In this adaptation, the reader can see that lines were omitted, but the reading of the scene flows and lends itself to the examining of a metaphor (love's wings) and character development: What risk has Romeo taken to be in the garden? Why does it matter? How will this risk impact Juliet's decision to meet him later?

As the scene plays out, there are so many questions for the reader in a writer's workshop to look at carefully regarding how the characters are designed by Shakespeare. Most importantly, the original language of the play, while altered, still retains its quality and tone, unlike many of the easy-read texts, and this version remains true to the author's intent.

When Romeo climbs to the balcony to meet Juliet, one is drawn not only to the youthful passion and daring but to the sound of Shakespeare's language, and one considers, too, how an author creates great characters. Now, having students "know" Shakespeare's

CHAPTER SEVEN

BOX 7.1

Romeo and Juliet. Act 2, Scene 2 (Adapted from *Reading about the World*, Volume 2, ed. Paul Brians)

(The following scene summary and text italics have been added.)

SCENE SUMMARY

Romeo, who was heartbroken over the breakup of his relationship with an older woman named Rosaline, needs some cheering up. His friends decide the Capulet's costume party is the way to meet new women, and they drag Romeo along. Romeo and his friends, who were not invited, attend the party knowing that if they are recognized, they might end up in a fight to the death with the Capulet family.

Later Romeo, in disguise, meets Juliet, who is also in costume. They form an instant attraction, hold hands, and sneak a kiss before the night is over, even though they never formally meet or see each other out of costume.

Romeo, who is now wildly attracted to Juliet, decides to leave his friends at the end of the evening and hang around in the Capulet's orchard, hoping to get another glimpse of Juliet. Later, Juliet steps out onto the balcony by her bedroom, reliving the meeting with Romeo, who she now knows is a Montague.

In this scene, Juliet says that although Romeo in name is her enemy, his body and flesh make him her love.

It is important to remember that the Capulets and Montagues are sworn enemies and have fought many times in the streets of the Italian city, Verona.

ROMEO AND JULIET. ACT 2, SCENE 2

[*Capulet's orchard.*]

ROMEO [*Coming forward.*]:
    But soft! What light (*do I see*) through yonder window breaks?
    It is the East, and Juliet is the sun!

It is my lady! O, it is my love!
O, that she knew she were! (*If Juliet only knew I loved her!*)
She speaks, yet she says nothing. (*Juliet is talking to herself.*)
What of that? I will answer it.
I am too bold; 'tis not to me she speaks. (*I'm wrong, she can't be thinking of me.*)
See how she leans her cheek upon her hand!
O, that I were a glove upon that hand,
That I might touch that cheek!

JULIET *[Sighing.]*:
　Ay me!

ROMEO *[Excited, surprised.]*:
　She speaks.
　O, speak again, bright angel, for thou art
　As glorious to this night
　As is a winged messenger of heaven (*Juliet, you're being here makes this is as wonderful a night as one might find in Heaven.*)

JULIET:
　O Romeo, Romeo! Wherefore (*Why*) art thou Romeo? (*Why must you be my enemy?*)
　Deny thy (*your*) father and refuse thy (*your*) name;
　Or, if not, be but sworn my love (*swear your love to me*),
　And I'll no longer be a Capulet (*I'll give up my name so that we could be together*).

ROMEO *[Aside.]*:
　Shall I hear more, or shall I speak at this?

JULIET:
　'Tis (*it is*) but thy name that is my enemy.
　Thou art thyself, though not a Montague. (*You are a person, not a name.*)

(continues)

BOX 7.1 (continued)

What's Montague? It is nor hand, nor foot,
Nor arm, nor face. O, be some other name
Belonging to a man (*If Romeo had a different name, she could be with him.*)
What's in a name? That which we call a rose
By any other word would smell as sweet.
Romeo, doff (*get rid of your*) thy name;
And
Take all myself.

ROMEO [*Speaking to Juliet from the shadow of darkness.*]:
I take thee at thy word (*and I'll change my name*).
Call me but love, and I'll be new baptized; (*Say you love me and I'll be a new man.*)
Henceforth I never will be Romeo. (*If you love me, we are no longer enemies.*)

JULIET:
What man art thou (*who are you?*), that, thus bescreened (*is hidden*) in night (*darkness*),
So stumblest (*invades*) on my counsel (*privacy*)?

ROMEO:
By a name
I know not how to tell thee (*you*) who I am.
My name, dear saint, is hateful to myself
Because it is an enemy to thee.
Had I it written, I would tear the word. (*I wish I could give myself a new name.*)

JULIET:
My ears have yet not drunk (*heard*) a hundred words
Of thy tongue's uttering, yet I know the sound (*Romeo's voice*).
Art thou not Romeo, and a Montague?

ROMEO:
> Neither, fair maid, if either thee dislike. (*I won't tell you my name if it will upset you.*)

JULIET:
> How camest thou hither, tell me, and wherefore? (*How did you get here? Why are you here?*)
> The orchard walls are high and hard to climb,
> And the place death, considering who thou art,
> If any of my kinsmen find thee here. (*If my cousins find you they will kill you.*)

ROMEO:
> With love's light wings did I o'erperch these walls; (*My love for you became wings, and I flew over these walls.*)
> For stony limits cannot hold love out, (*Nothing, not even stone walls, can keep love away.*)
> And what love can do, that dares love attempt. (*Love gives one the power to do anything.*)
> Therefore thy kinsmen are no stop to me. (*Love makes me fear no one.*)

JULIET:
> If they do see thee, they will murder thee.

ROMEO:
> Alack, there (*is*) more peril (*danger*) in thine (*your*) eye
> Than twenty of their swords! Look thou but sweet, (*I'm more afraid you don't love me.*)
> And I am proof against their enmity. (*If you love me, I am safe from my enemies.*)

JULIET:
> I would not (*wish*) for the world they saw thee here.

(continues)

CHAPTER SEVEN

> **BOX 7.1 (continued)**
>
> ROMEO:
> I have night's cloak (*darkness*) to hide me from their eyes;
> And but thou love me, let them find me here. (*If you don't love me, let them find me.*)
> My life were better ended by their (*your cousin's*) hate
> Than death prorogued, wanting of thy love. (*I'm better off dead than living without your love.*)
>
> (*End of adapted excerpt.*)

play takes on an entirely new dimension when taught from the perspective of a writer.

No longer are students reading to understand plot or to identify literary devices; they are using their writers' eyes to see how the bard brought all of his creative powers to bear when fleshing out these timeless lovers. Through reading key scenes, students evaluate character, tension, plot, irony, and many other elements of great fiction and ask themselves if there are any lessons that can apply to their own writings. And, of course, there are many.

The teacher and students can talk about motivation and how they know it; they can predict and then read on with purpose; they can try to understand what the timelessness of the play might be and how it relates to present day; and they do this all with specific references. Text references make opinions valid, and students have informed discussions. They are, as Frank Smith posits, "reading like writers," and the evaluating of the play generates depths of thinking that one can only hope for when literature is approached from a traditional teacher posture.

It may seem controversial to pare down these works, especially when one looks through the American literature packets (Boxes 7.2, 7.3, and 7.4) provided, but experience shows that when students get these works in small, manageable doses, they often want to read more.

BOX 7.2
American Literature/
Hawthorne and Melville/Packet I

Hawthorne and Melville were concerned with the dark side of human nature. Hawthorne wrote about religion and its emphasis on sin and the soul. In the "Minister's Black Veil," Hawthorne writes about the Puritans' religious fixation with sin and the impact that obsessing over sin has on one's emotional and mental well-being. In *Moby Dick*, Melville creates Captain Ahab, a man obsessed with revenge on a whale that he blames for the disfigurement of his face and leg. Both of these stories are *allegories*, which means that many aspects of the stories—setting, characters, and plot—have symbolic meaning. Allegories are stories that refer to larger issues in life and present philosophical ideas for the reader to consider.

Note: Both parts of this assignment are to be done completely. No partial credit will be given.

Part I: "The Minister's Black Veil" is the story of a clergyman who covers his face with a black veil, causing the townspeople to eventually shun and dislike him. Beginning with the line, "The minister of Westbury approached the bedside..." on page 326, read to the ending of the story. In this closing scene, the minister asks the dying clergyman, Mr. Hooper, to remove the veil from his face "[b]efore the veil of eternity be lifted..." meaning that before you die, let me take this off your face, but Hooper refuses.

Directions: After reading the passage, answer the following questions. Please write in complete sentences and use "quoted" examples to support your answers.

1. Why would Hooper refuse to take the veil off? What does the veil mean to him? [*Key passage*: "'When a friend shows his inmost heart ... on every visage a Black Veil!'" (327). Try reading

(continues)

CHAPTER SEVEN

> **BOX 7.2 (*continued*)**
>
> this passage without the word "when" where it is used.] *Words to know: loathsomely*—hatefully; *affrighted*—fearful; *obscurity*—from nowhere; *visage*—face.
> 2. In the key passage, where Hooper talks about the veil as a symbol—an idea represented by something real—what is Hooper saying the black veil represents?
> 3. The ending line of the story deals with the grass growing above the minister's grave and the "awful thought" of the black veil buried beneath it. Here, the buried veil is like the hidden sins in someone's heart. What would this ending suggest is the theme of this story? (Think about Hooper and his willingness to wear the veil and never take it off.)

Part 2: Moby Dick is considered the finest American novel ever written because of the wide range of ideas, character development, and writing. (Ironically, Melville self-published the book and it was ridiculed by the critics of his day. Only after his death was the book read and praised.) It is an intense novel, which centers on Captain Ahab and his obsession with killing a white whale named Moby Dick.

Directions: Read from page 334, "'Captain Ahab,' said Starbuck," to page 335, "God keep me!—Keep us all!" and answer the questions related to this passage. In this scene, Ahab is "pumping up" the crew to help him find and kill the white whale. [*Key passage*: "All visible objects are but pasteboard masks ... white whale in principle." Ahab says here that although the whale has no human qualities and never meant to harm him, he is still a prisoner of what the whale symbolizes, which is the pain, humiliation, and suffering Ahab has endured since the whale disfigured him. Ahab no longer feels perfect and is now less of a man because of his injuries.] *Words to know: accursed*—damned; *razzed*—tore down, hurt; *imprecations*—gestures or actions that bring about evil; *maelstrom*—great whirlpool; *incense*—anger; *doltish*—dumb, unimaginative; *pagan*—not religious; *indignity*—insult; *torrid*—hot, focused;

> *perdition*—hell; *grog*—alcoholic drink; *vengeance*—revenge; *smite*—hit, strike; *enraged*—angry; *blasphemous*—against the laws of nature or God; *malice*—hate; *inscrutable*—mysterious, hard to understand; *sinewing*—laced with; *whetstone*—sharpening wheel; *constrainings*—limits; *fiends*—devils; *"a little lower"*—explained simply.
>
> 1. In the following quote, Ahab says, in effect, don't tell me what I can or cannot do: "I'd strike the sun if it insulted me." This statement is an example of the Greek word *hubris*, which means excessive pride. How does Ahab's pride affect his thinking about the whale and the purpose of the trip? (Pay attention to Starbuck's comments.)
> 2. Starbuck is the only member of the crew to challenge Ahab. What does Starbuck say and does it make sense for the crew and the ship?
> 3. Critics of *Moby Dick* feel that Starbuck is the conscience that Ahab has lost. Would you agree? Why?
>
> Be sure to check your answers, handwriting, and spelling before turning this assignment in for a grade.

During self-directed reading, some students pick up more of Walt Whitman or Henry Thoreau to read, having developed the confidence and, more importantly, the interest in them. Again, the key is interest and confidence when it comes to student literacy and the perpetuation of the classics.

Any student who is not engaged in the intensity of thought and writing that the classics require will never read them outside of school, so just teaching what they "mean" through class discussion and lecture is a waste of time; no one is inspired to read or write, and no one will ever be singed by the life-affirming fire of creativity.

In Box 7.2 the students do not read the entire short story but only the excerpts identified in the packet. The purpose is to focus on a particular literary concept and expose them to the writing of the period. Also provided here are three literature packets designed for the American literature series, *American Experience in Literature: Timeless Voices, Timeless Themes* (Prentice-Hall), in the event that they may be adaptable to a school district's anthology.

Writing, and reading like writers, provides the context required for the teaching of literature. To facilitate the building of context in any class, a teacher should not only think about what it is that students can get from the works of the anthologized authors, but also what students can learn from some of the living greats.

Russell Banks's *Cloudsplitter* (Box 7.5) is a reading and writing activity that considers the following question: How does one write about what exists only in the mind or heart? Banks's writing in this excerpt is extraordinary, fits in nicely with an American literature class, exposes students to thinking about reading and writing at a complex level, reinforces reading skills, and relates to their creative endeavors as well.

When designing context with general literature classes, it is important to review the anthology and look at what can be culled from it, particularly with a higher theme or goal that can be carried through the school year.

Are there themes of isolation, independence, or courage that can become the overriding structure of the class? Can a piece from one's writing folder also have a theme, idea, plot line or convention, conflict, resolution, or setting that is similar to a story that was read? (Again, this eventually makes for a great final exam question: What have you written this year that has at least three characteristics similar to a story we've read as a class? Please cite specific examples from both to support your opinion.)

Identifying a theme for the year gives purpose and reference points that link reading and writing. (Ironic, isn't it, that reading is often taught as a separate discipline from writing? Many middle schools have a reading block distinct from a writing block and the two have no relation to each other.)

The role of the teacher is to keep an eye out for similarities in students' reading and writing as it relates to the larger teaching context.

BOX 7.3
American Literature/
Emerson, Thoreau, and Whitman/Packet 2

All three writers believed in independent thinking and trusting one's judgment, and all stressed an appreciation for nature as a way to find purpose, beauty, and meaning in life. They were reacting to the scientific movement, which stated that all of the mysteries of life could be explained through scientific study.

Note: All parts of this assignment are to be done completely. No partial credit will be given. As always, answer all questions in complete sentences and use "quotes" to support your answer.

Directions: Read from "Whoso be a man ..." to "To be great is to be misunderstood ..." on pages 366–67, from "Self-Reliance" by Emerson. He says in this passage that while society has its good points, it requires that everyone think and act the same in order to survive, which stifles creativity, independence, and genius. This is a difficult passage to read, but some obvious ideas are present. Essentially, these paragraphs deal with the risks of speaking your mind and being different. [*Key passage:* "A foolish consistency ... divines" (367). Emerson says here that always believing in the same popular ideas without question might work for politicians, philosophers, or priests, but what about the independent thinker who wants to see the world differently?] *Words to know: non-conformist*—not affected by popular thought or culture; *integrity*—personal honesty; *contradict*—argue against; *hindered*—slowed down; *"gather immortal palms"*—do great things.

1. Why does Emerson argue for men (and women!) to be different?
2. "To be great is to be misunderstood...." What does Emerson say here about the risks of being an independent thinker and is what he says of any value in today's society?

(continues)

CHAPTER SEVEN

> **BOX 7.3 (continued)**
>
> Read from "I learned this, at least . . ." to "Now put the foundations under them . . ." on pages 377–78, from the conclusion of *Walden* by Thoreau. He tells the reader what he has learned from turning his back on society and living in isolation for two years in a cabin by Walden Pond. This is the "experiment" he refers to in the first line of the passage. *Words to know: endeavor*—try; *"unexpected in common hours"*—beyond the ordinary; *boundary*—limits; *liberal*—better, less limiting; *interpreted*—changed; *"with a license of a higher order of beings"*—have the chance to develop a higher purpose for living one's life; *"and solitude will not be solitude"*—you will not be alone and will understand what it is to live in a better world.
>
> 1. How is this passage similar in thought to Emerson's ideas? What do both men say that is the same?
> 2. Thoreau mentions "castles in the air." What does this mean in terms of how one plans for the future?
>
> Read "When I Heard the Learn'd Astronomer" on page 415 by Walt Whitman. Whitman shares the views of Thoreau and Emerson about science being no substitute for appreciating and experiencing nature.
>
> 1. What is Whitman's reaction to the "Learn'd" astronomer's presentation about the stars? [*Words to know: unaccountable*—for no reason; *learn'd*—knowledgeable, used here sarcastically.]
> 2. What does it matter that he prefers to look at the stars instead of talking about them?

Many times impromptu literature circles formed around the reading and writing observations of students will add clarity and meaning to what was, or may be, read. Connecting literature to writing creates an ongoing thinking loop that deepens and enriches understanding about fiction and one's literate abilities, and by

BOX 7.4
American Literature/
Fitzgerald and Hemingway/Packet 3

Directions: Read the passages (attached) from F. Scott Fitzgerald's "Winter Dreams" (number 1 and 2) and *Great Gatsby* (number 1 only). Both stories deal with young men during the Roaring Twenties, a time of wealth and prosperity. From these passages, answer the following questions. As always, answer in complete sentences with quoted passages from the text to support your opinion. *No partial credit will be given—all questions must be answered.*

1. How are Dexter (in "Winter Dreams") and Jay Gatsby (in *The Great Gatsby*) similar? What are their ambitions, dreams, and hopes?
2. Why are the women, Judy Jones ("WD") and Daisy Buchanan (GG), so desired by Dexter and Jay? What does Fitzgerald intend for them to symbolize for the reader? (A symbol is an idea represented by something real. For example, the flag represents freedom.)
3. What point about life during the twenties is Fitzgerald making by having both relationships fail? (Hint: Think about how and why these men made careers for themselves and why loving these women meant so much to them.)

Read passage number 2 from *The Great Gatsby*. This short excerpt also gives the reader an idea of Fitzgerald's tone for the overall telling of the novel. Tone reflects the attitude the author takes when telling the story. What is the narrator saying about the rich? What would you say the tone of this story is?

Read passage number 3 from *Great Gatsby*. It is one of the most well-known novel endings ever written, and it reconsiders Gatsby's buying a house across the bay from Daisy's. At the end of the book, the

(continues)

CHAPTER SEVEN

> **BOX 7.4 (*continued*)**
>
> narrator wonders what must have gone through Gatsby's mind when he looked across the water at her home and dock.
>
> 1. What is your first reaction to it? Does it seem to you like the book ends happily? Why or why not?
> 2. What does this ending tell the reader about chasing after a life built on money and fame to impress others?
> 3. The last few lines deal with the never-ending dreams we all have about being rich and famous. Fitzgerald writes that even though it's a one-in-a-million shot, we continue to hope our efforts to be rich will come true and we "beat on ... borne back ceaselessly into the past." What is Fitzgerald saying about human nature? Why do we keep dreaming, and how does it affect us—according to Fitzgerald—if the dream never comes true?
> 4. In general, from all these excerpts, you could argue that Fitzgerald writes of a time when life was focused on the superficial—money, image, and fame. Is this true from what you've read, and how has present-day living changed since the 1920s?
>
> Read all of "In Another Country" (pages 731–34 in the literature book) by Ernest Hemingway. It is the story of a few World War I veterans in a rehabilitation hospital in Italy. The narrator, who is trying to regain the muscle strength in his legs, is the only American in the ward.
>
> 1. What the reader learns about the Italian general is ironic and tragic, meaning that it was both sad and the opposite of what you'd expect (ironic). What does the reader learn about the general and how does it support the previous statement?
> 2. Compare the writing style of Hemingway to that of Fitzgerald. How are they different? Use the passages you have to compare the two writers.
> 3. The title "In Another Country" has a literal and figurative meaning. Literally, which means as it is written, the American GI is phys-

> ically a long way from home. Figuratively, the title also gives the reader an idea about the main character's emotions and reflects upon to the GI's relationship with the other men in the ward. What is his relationship with the other patients, and how does the title serve more than just one meaning? (Hint: Does being an American make him different and alone?)

grounding these connections in work that matters to the class, learning is made purposeful and richer.

Ultimately, a teacher needs to be more observant of what he or she sees and hears in the classroom on a daily basis. The instructor comes to trust that many of the week's lessons will eventually grow out of the understanding, skills, and needs that the class presents in the ongoing process of becoming more sophisticated in literacy.

Another way to use literature in the classroom is to find short passages that can teach a concept to a student independently (Box 7.6). The advantage to these short passages is that a student who is ahead of the others can work on these for extra credit freeing the teacher to spend more time with those who need it. Because the excerpts are short and self-explanatory, students generally enjoy doing them (and they are from books that a student might find in a bookstore, serving as "teasers" in that they might encourage a student to pick up the book), and simplify concepts.

In both of these examples, students get enough information to look at concepts independently, and they look closely at literature, use of language, writing style, and word choice in manageable and readable formats. Developing these for a workshop class should be part of a teacher's planning.

CHAPTER SEVEN

> **BOX 7.5**
> **Writing Details into a Story**
>
> One of the qualities of great writing is the use of specific detail to make readers feel like they are a part of the story. Writing about just the right details makes the story seem real to the reader because it helps the reader "see" what's happening in his or her mind. Russell Banks's novel, *Cloudsplitter*, is an excellent example of the writing of details to provide the reader with a sense of time, place, and emotion.
>
> *Cloudsplitter* is the story of John Brown, an abolitionist, as told through the eyes of his grown son, Owen. In this passage from pages 108–12, Owen is writing to his father John (the letter is placed in *italics* by the author) about the death of his little stepsister, Kitty. Ruth, an older sister, is responsible for Kitty's death. Owen also tells the reader of his younger brother, Fred, and of his stepmother, Mary.
>
> *Directions:*
>
> *Part 1:* Please read the passage and, in your Writer's Notebook, write your reaction to it. What did you feel or think about as you read?
>
> *Part 2:* Please reread the passage to do the following: In your Writer's Notebook, make a list of all the details that create a picture in your mind.
>
> *Part 3:* In groups of three, share your list of details. Were there any differences to what others noted? Any similarities?
>
> As a group, does the letter to the father relate the same emotion as what Owen tells the reader? Why or why not?
>
> *Essay question:* What details in the story made it seem real for you? Please give three examples to support your answer. This essay is worth ten As. Also, you need to stay focused during the group discussion or you could earn a grade that will make you unhappy.

BOX 7.6
Setting and Character Development

Setting: The physical place(s) in a story. The setting influences the action, mood, or thinking of a character.

Directions: As you read this excerpt from chapter 2 of Tim O'Brien's *Going after Cacciato*, consider how the author uses the quiet setting of a sentry post or lookout tower to share with the reader how Paul Berlin thinks and what he likes to do when he is alone. Please answer the essay question below.

Essay Question: Does the description of the setting fit the mood of the main character and does it help us understand what Paul likes to think about when he is alone? This is worth 8 As.

Key to understanding the excerpt: This passage is from a novel about the Vietnam War and a group of soldiers out on patrol near a beach.

THE OBSERVATION POST

Paul Berlin, whose only goal in life was to live long enough to establish goals worth living for still longer, stood high in the tower by the sea, the night soft around him, and wondered, not for the first time, about the immense powers of his imagination. A truly awesome notion. Not a dream. An idea to develop, to tinker with and build and sustain, to draw out his visions.

He checked his watch. It was not quite midnight.

For a time he stood quietly at the tower's north wall, looking out to where the beach jagged sharply into the sea to form a natural barrier against storms. The night was quiet. On the sand below, coils of barbed wire circled the observation tower in a perimeter that separated it from the rest of the war. The tripflares were out. Things were in place. Beside him, Harold Murphy's machine gun was fully loaded and ready, and a dozen signal flares were

(continues)

BOX 7.6 (continued)

lined up on the wall, and the radio was working, and the beach was mined, and the tower itself was high and strong and fortified. The sea guarded his rear. The moon gave light. It would be all right, he told himself. He was safe.

He lighted a cigarette and moved to the west wall.

Doc and Eddie and Oscar and the others slept peacefully. And the night was peaceful. Time to consider the possibilities.

Another example comes from *Harry Potter and the Sorcerer's Stone*:

AUTHOR'S VOICE AND WRITING STYLE

Author's Voice: How an author uses words to create an effect, emotion, or attitude that is based on the author's writing style.

Directions: Read the following excerpt from *Harry Potter and the Sorcerer's Stone* by J. K. Rowling and answer the essay question below using the basic essay format.

Essay: What feeling or attitude does the author's voice create in the opening of this passage? This assignment is worth 5 As.

CHAPTER 1: THE BOY WHO LIVED

Mr. and Mrs. Dursley, of number four, Privet Drive, were proud to say that they were perfectly normal, thank you very much. They were the last people you'd expect to be involved in anything strange or mysterious, because they just didn't hold with such nonsense.

CHAPTER EIGHT
PERFORMANCE-BASED EXAMS

Essentially, the week or two a school shuts down to administer exams is a tremendous waste of time. Many educators rely on the all-encompassing comprehensive exam and dutifully use a Scantron grid sheet because they believe it holds a number of questions that can validate what is taught and measure what was learned. Neither of course is true, but ignorance of assessment and lack of understanding about authentic learning dominate the profession and support the exam model of learning.

It is time to use exam week as learning time, to keep up the momentum built into a workshop class, and to authentically measure the depth of understanding that students have developed about reading and writing. The performance-based exam is actually a series of reading and writing activities that expand upon the comprehension, thinking, and writing skills all students have developed. Students are asked to reflect on their progress as readers, writers, thinkers, and learners—goals that were considered and generated in the first quarter. (The designing of goals is explained in chapter 9.)

An exam for a workshop class can have vocabulary, grammar, and literature sections that ask multiple "guess" or short-answer questions.

CHAPTER EIGHT

If the exam has four parts, then each is graded as A, F, or 0. Determine, for example, that out of the twenty questions in a part, fifteen to sixteen correct answers is an A, seventeen to eighteen an A+ (95) and nineteen to twenty was an A++ (100). Mathematically, fifteen correct out of twenty is an 80 percent score, and fourteen out of twenty is a 75, but anything less than fifteen correct is graded as a 60, so there's more pressure on the students to score well. Later, all four sections are graded and averaged for a total exam score.

Over time, one might prefer an exam that reinforces the major reading and writing skills taught by applying them to new material, one that compares pieces of literature, pulls together concepts that have been worked on in class, and expands upon self-evaluation or reflection of student work and progress toward personal literacy goals.

Over a week of classes, students can tackle a different section and turn in their work to the instructor. Unless a student truly misunderstands a part of the test, most of the work is generally well done and of quality. Remember, too, that the grading is A, F, or 0, which requires essays without major errors in paragraphing, text references, grammar, factual evidence, or mechanics—such essays or responses do earn an F, so there is little margin for error.

During the exam cycle, the skills learned through collaboration with the teacher and a student's peers have to be demonstrated. Box 8.1 is an example of a performance-based midterm exam.

The building of a summative portfolio is the culmination of the year's work based on the goals designed in the beginning. Pulling a portfolio together makes students focus on what was learned and what their strengths were, creating a visible documentation of quality work that sums up the year much better than an exam ever could.

Whereas a traditional exam is heavy on fact retention, a portfolio is an authentic demonstration of facts and skills in an applied

> **BOX 8.1**
> **Midterm Exam C period 9H**
>
> **DIRECTIONS:**
>
> *Part One.* Do not write on the exam. You are to read the chapter excerpt from *Naked* by David Sedaris, entitled "A Plague of Tics," and do a book evaluation essay. "A Plague of Tics" is about Sedaris's life as a young boy. In this excerpt, he struggles with Obsessive Compulsive Disorder (OCD), but he manages to find humor in his condition.
>
> *Part Two.* Early in *Great Expectations* Miss Havisham says to Pip, "Play the game out," during a card game. At the time, Pip disliked Estella and no longer wanted to stay and visit, but Havisham made him. As the novel continues, this sentence has greater and greater significance. How does this phrase mirror the future for Pip and Estella? What are the "games" Pip and Estella will play as they grow into adults, and how will it shape their lives? Be sure to use proper essay format and give two examples for each character from the story to support your opinion. You may use the textbook to find supporting evidence. (Hint: Your essay will be at least six paragraphs long.)
>
> *Bonus.* In "A Plague of Tics" the boy does not seem to see the disease as others do. Find two examples of how others view him and then compare how they see him to how he feels about himself.
>
> *Grades:* 100, 95, 90, 60, or 0. Each section will be graded separately and the scores will be combined.

learning construct; all the work in a portfolio documents not only learning but also sophisticated thinking, effort, and learned skills.

A final exam (Box 8.2) that has students reflect upon what was learned is a thinking activity and not just an exercise in recall. The

CHAPTER EIGHT

BOX 8.2
Cover Sheet—Grade 11 Final Exam

General Directions: All sheets needed to complete this exam will be provided to you. Be sure to put your name on every sheet of paper. The grades for all four sections are 100, 95, 60, or 0—depending on the quality of your essay.

PART 1

Directions: Answer the following: *What defines the American personality and to which American writers can this personality be traced?*

PART 2: *GREAT EXPECTATIONS/GREAT GATSBY* ANALYSIS

Directions: Read the excerpts from The Great Gatsby and Great Expectations, then answer the following questions. Use proper essay format.

Question 1: Read excerpt 1 from The Great Gatsby and excerpt 3 from Great Expectations. *How is Jay Gatsby's motivation in life the same as Pip's, and how is Jay's life experience in the passage similar to Pip's?* Note: Be sure to *briefly* summarize each excerpt in the second paragraph of your essay.

Question 2: Read excerpt 4 from Great Expectations and 3 from The Great Gatsby. The house that Pip admired as a boy is not unlike the house Jay Gatsby admired from across the bay. Both novels end leaving the reader with a feeling of sadness for what might have been for Jay and Pip had their lives worked out as they had hoped. *Please determine what each house meant for the two men and how the reader was left with a sense that their hopes were never realized.*

Note: Consider the two women mentioned in *all* the excerpts, how the authors described them, and what they meant to Pip and Jay as you consider your response. Looking at the women in these excerpts can help you draw conclusions about the ending of both novels and the tone set by the authors.

PART 3

Some novels have slow points or lulls in them. From the notes made in your Writer's Notebook about the books you've read, *discuss how one book may or may not have had a lull and provide an example of how this speaks to the planning and writing of the novel. Be sure to briefly summarize the plot of the book and provide examples from your notebook to support your opinion.*

PART 4: MARTIN LUTHER KING'S "I HAVE A DREAM" SPEECH

Directions: Read the excerpt from Martin Luther King's "I Have a Dream" speech and answer the following question: *How do King's words, ideas, and/or actions represent the thinking and writing of at least two of the authors we've looked at in American literature?*

---

exam presented below is graded as 20 percent of the final course grade—as mandated by the school district.

The remaining 80 percent of the final grade was determined by the final portfolio grade (Box 8.3). The following demonstrates what was required and how the class prepared (Box 8.4) to meet the expectations.

The portfolio and the final exam are far removed from a traditional exam and require a tremendous amount of effort, quality, and thinking. The grade received is much more meaningful and is a true document of student learning and growth. As one can see, it requires much planning from midyear and on, but this gives the course a day-to-day focus and momentum for learning.

BOX 8.3
Finished Portfolio Grade Sheet

A++ (100) All work with at least an A grade as specified by Second-Term Assignment Checklist (Box 8.4), including extra credit options, is complete with at least three fourths (combined) of the papers in the portfolio having an A++ or A+ grade, *or all extra credit assignments are included* and have an A grade. See Grade Scale for Academic Writing for grade criteria (page 63).

A+ (95) Same as above in terms of requirements of Second-Term Assignment Checklist, with a quarter of the papers having at least an A+ grade, *or half of all extra credit assignments are included* and have an A grade. *Note:* An A++ grade can be earned if *all extra credit assignments are included* and have an A grade.

A (90) Same as above in terms of requirements of Second-Term Assignment Checklist, with all papers having an A grade, including extra credit options. *Note:* An A+ portfolio can be earned if *half of all extra credit assignments are included* and have an A grade. *This grade is the expected goal of the semester's work. Any student that completes work on time and with reasonable effort should earn this grade.*

Note: No portfolio can have a 90 grade or higher if any of the following assignments have not earned an A grade: either of the two book evaluation essays or one compare-and-contrast essay. Also, *a student who has successfully completed the Second-Term Assignment Sheet can move up one or two grades by completing half (a 95 grade) or all (a 100 grade) of the extra credit available.*

PERFORMANCE-BASED EXAMS

F (60)	Book evaluation or compare-and-contrast essays are missing (have not received an A grade)—no extra credit can be substituted for these—or 10 percent of Second-Term Assignment Sheet pieces are not done or are missing.
0	Less than half of the required assignments for Second-Term Assignment Sheet are done and have an A grade.

A portfolio with a grade of 90 percent represents the required work of the course. As you place completed assignments in portfolios, they will earn credit for your final portfolio grade.

BOX 8.4
Second-Term Assignment Checklist

Directions: The following assignments *must be done* in order to receive an *A* grade for the final portfolio. *Any work missing will result in an F* (60).

Name: _____ Date: _____

Book evaluation essay (green sheet) #1 turned in ___ final grade ___

Book evaluation essay (green sheet) #2 turned in ___ final grade ___

Compare and contrast (gold sheet) turned in _____ final grade _____

Go Ask Alice essay turned in _____ final grade _____

Romeo and Juliet essay turned in _____ final grade _____

Pearl essay turned in _____ final grade _____

Vocabulary sheets 4, 5, and practice test: complete ___ incomplete ___

In addition, the Writer's Notebook *daily journal* and all *Two-Page* assignments are *up to date.* Your portfolio should contain *one writing piece* that includes *first, second, and final drafts*, and you may add any other item of your choice.

FINAL PORTFOLIO CHECKLIST

A+ portfolio (95) must contain the items listed above *and* the following:

Another Compare and Contrast essay; (choose *one*) Book Link, Author's Theme, or Characters and Conflict assignment; *also,* the *Odyssey* essay; and a choice of any *three* from the following: *They Cage Animals at Night, Naked, Child Called 'It',* "Observation Post," *Dead School, Harry Potter and the Sorcerer's Stone, Tuesdays with Morrie, Tripwire, The God of Small Things,* or *When Legends Die,* excerpts.

A++ portfolio (100) must have the work listed for an A+ portfolio *and* the following:

(Choose *two*) Book Link, Author's Theme, or Characters and Conflict assignment; *also,* the *Odyssey* essay; and any *six* from the following: *They Cage Animals at Night, Naked, Child Called 'It',* "Observation Post," *Dead School, Harry Potter and the Sorcerer's Stone, Tuesdays with Morrie, Tripwire, The God of Small Things,* or *When Legends Die,* excerpts.

If you have a question about extra credit, see *me.* You can add an extra credit assignment of your own in place of one listed, *after we discuss it.*

CHAPTER NINE
WRITING THE RESEARCH PAPER

Of all the lessons that are taught in an English class, the research paper is the most involved, intense, and difficult for both teachers and students. In many ways the format, grading, explanation of the paper, topic choice, requirements, length, bibliography, and citations are major hurdles to writing coherent and thoughtful papers. Students are many times overwhelmed simply by the directions and are satisfied just to pass.

Fortunately, using the writing workshop model improves the process considerably since the paper is worked on step by step so that many problems can be avoided and the amount of instructional time devoted to the project is justified.

A critical paper organized in the following format—cover page, table of contents, introduction, statement of problem (thesis), review of literature, summary, conclusion, and bibliography—in MLA style is perfect for a workshop class because it can be done in segments and is in a critical analysis format that is easy to set up and work through with students.

One can adopt this setup for research writing for the workshop class, minus the summary (redundant for a shorter paper). Sharing quality papers written by former students and spending some time showing the class how the paper will look by leafing through a student copy will help them understand the intended written form for their completed work.

Getting Started with a Few Small Changes

Generally, the traditional process of writing a paper begins with a trip to the school library where the librarian, in consultation with the teacher, has dutifully amassed a set of books and topics for students to explore. Students sift through the piles of materials set aside and try to decide, in most cases, what would be easiest to write about in relation to the assignment. Rather than having a choice, they are forced to consider subjects that sound impressive (early American authors, the Transcendentalists) but are not the least bit interesting.

Is it any wonder that the research paper becomes an exercise in semiplagiarized futility? Thankfully, a few small changes make a huge difference.

Identifying the topics about which students might like to write, and what they might learn from doing so, is at the heart of a good research activity. It is always a good idea to brainstorm with the class a list of ideas that matter to them before even discussing the expected, written format or consulting with the librarian.

Students always surprise me with their topics: family illnesses, body image, tattoos, illegal drugs, the death penalty and the prison system, pornography, poverty, race, the media, gender, and conservation—among others—after just a short thinking session.

Once they settle on an idea, then they decide what it is about the topic that needs to be researched. It is best to frame this next step as a "problem" (rather than a thesis), in the sense that there must be something about the topic that is controversial or unknown to the reader of the paper. For example, why do you want to write about media and girls? Why should people not smoke in public? Why doesn't the death penalty work, or does it?

Once students consider these questions and formulate ideas, then they are ready to create the statement of the problem section of their paper and the focal point of their research (thesis). Generating a problem statement is easier for students to understand than developing a thesis, which is a vacuous and unfocused concept for those new to research writing. Having a problem to present or solve is easier for the teacher to explain and for the student to write about and research purposefully.

At this point, they then read a model introduction and statement of the problem (Box 9.1) and learn the difference between the two. Obviously, in the introduction, the reader is given a sense about why the pupil has an interest in the topic, while the statement is what the author will discuss.

It is important to remember that research is about critical thinking, not just "looking stuff up," as some savvier students have noted. It is about accessing the right information, considering a wide variety of learned opinions, and then forming a coherent and logical conclusion. It is important to raise this point because all research is ultimately done from a critical perspective—no one ever just "looks up stuff."

When students are engaged in a subject, they have a plan for tackling the paper and managing the volumes of research material available to them. The task—fueled by their interest in the topic—becomes possible and the emphasis shifts to organizing, writing one's ideas in logical order, and forming a critical opinion based on proper research. In effect, the writing becomes something that *can* be done by the student, as opposed to what can be cobbled together—and generally plagiarized—to get a passing grade.

Research is an important skill to teach correctly—this cannot be emphasized enough. Once during a peer edit with a very bright, college-bound senior, we discussed how properly done research allows one to become part of the greater intellectual landscape—something not even considered when struggling to *just get the damn thing done.*

This student's thesis was on autobiographical writing; she was exploring whether or not one can truly trust the author of an auto-

BOX 9.1
Research Paper

INTRODUCTION

Teenage pregnancy is an issue that I have been interested in since the best friend of my older sister had a child while she was still in high school. I saw how hard it was for her and her family to have a baby around the house. She hardly ever went out, had to work, study, and take care of a baby. The worst part was that she broke up with her boyfriend, and he was ordered by the court to provide child support, but it wasn't enough and she had a hard time.

I hope to learn more about teenage pregnancy and how it can be avoided.

STATEMENT OF THE PROBLEM

As of 1998, 149,000 junior high girls became pregnant every year in the United States (Author's last name, page number). This statistic does not include high school girls!

The effects of these pregnancies are devastating in terms of a young girl's education, career possibilities, and potential happiness, and it takes an emotional toll on a teen's family as well. Research suggests that sexual abstinence can reduce teen pregnancy significantly, but does it work for junior high girls? Are there other methods to consider, including sex education classes at the middle or junior high level that might work more practically and deal more thoroughly with the issues that surround teen pregnancy? The goal of this paper is to find the best method to help young women make positive decisions about their personal relationships and their bodies.

Note the obvious difference between the introduction and the statement of the problem. What is the difference between the two?

biography since, of the different books she had read, some seemed more realistic than others (this was before *A Million Little Pieces* by James Frey was published), and she wanted to explore the writing and biographical history of each book and author.

During a peer edit, she realized that this paper was a way of adding her voice to those of others who care enough to discuss how we define honest writing—in this case, of the autobiography. It was a nice moment for both of us to think that there was a greater purpose here than just to complete a school assignment.

Beginning, Again, to Write

Students begin to write the research paper just as they had begun writing on the first few days of class, by creating lists of items that matter to them, so the class is not moving on to an assignment that is so different that the workshop routine has to be dropped. The research paper is an extension of what the class is used to doing inasmuch as once topics are identified and research is gathered, then the workshop process can begin. (At this point, a focus lesson about the credibility of websites is in order.)

Once students have a statement of the problem and the sources they plan to use, the next step is to ask students to create writer's outlines for the documentation phase of the paper, or the review of literature. Because it is the most difficult part to write correctly in terms of quotations, citations, organization, coherence, and relevance, an outline is a must.

An outline can be organized in many different ways, but the best way to help each individual writer is to focus on the main points that have surfaced from the research and what lasting impression or opinion has formed as a result. A statement of the problem that considered whether secondhand smoke was dangerous or not may have a number of competing views, and, hopefully, the student will have formed an opinion as well. The outline then would begin with those views that are in opposition to the writer's and finish with those that support the writer's.

In essence, one has a two-tiered process for writing now, and the outline should look like this:

Review of the Literature Outline

Name: _____ Date: _____

Statement of Problem:

_____

_____

Directions: Based on your *teacher-approved* statement, organize the outline below by listing facts from the *least* compelling or supportive to the most. Remember, each fact must be referred to by page and author in your written review.

1. _____

2. _____

And lines are added until the list is complete. At the end, the writer adds this to form a brief conclusion: "From the research I decided that this is what is most important, proven, or most likely to be true about my topic."

Once the outline is reviewed, have students use a marker to highlight key words, sentences, or passages in their research so that as they prepare to write, they will remember the main points they've selected. Surprisingly, students who use index cards or who don't highlight what they feel is important from an article tend to lose their way when they write, probably because when sitting down later, they have to reinvent their trains of thought and sometimes lose what it was in the first place that compelled them to include a reference.

CHAPTER NINE

The outline and the highlighting make the actual writing flow better, and a student's voice is much more likely to appear when the focus is on what is to be said rather than why it was said.

What is important to note about the outline's organization is that it must begin with one focal point, the statement of the problem, and end with another, a draft conclusion. Having this, along with highlighted reference material, gives the writer a very easy and comfortable structure within which to begin.

The drafting of the review is done in class over the course of a few days, which allows the teacher the opportunity to sit in on the process and stay in the loop. Having students write this section at home, along with other aspects of the paper, will only frustrate both teacher and writer. All good progress made in class will be lost in the returned, written-at-home versions. Because research writing is intense, it is better when done in class so that problems can be noticed, questions answered, corrections made immediately, and focus maintained.

To make the in-class process more efficient, students are given peer-editing checklists and a research paper style sheet that is a quick reference for formatting and mechanics (Box 9.2). Establishing both style and peer-editing sheets places expectations for writing and revising in the open; students cannot claim that they did something wrong because they weren't aware of how it was to be done. They have writing models and subsequent directions, as listed in the style sheet, for example (Box 9.2).

Once a draft is written and peer-reviewed, it is turned in for a first reading, which the instructor corrects and comments on. The draft is then returned to the student for either a quick conference or a longer one, if needed. The review of literature is rewritten correctly and then meets the criteria for the assignment. Since the Skinner grading model of A, F, or 0 is used, all revisions are expected to reach an A level, just as with all sections of the paper.

Students who choose not to revise to an A level can take an F for this section, as they can for any other. The grading of the paper

BOX 9.2
Research Paper Style Sheet

The following is a list to keep in mind when typing up and preparing the final copy of your paper.

- One space after a period or a comma.
- Place the end punctuation—usually a period—after the citation if it ends the sentence. For example, "Body image affects self-worth (Author's last name, page number)." Also, place the period inside the end quote if there is no citation at the end of the sentence: "Girl Talk."
- Name and page number are on the top of each page of your report.
- When using more than four lines directly from a primary source, type it as

(Example) Frank Smith in *Further Essays into Education* writes,

> Anything a child is not interested in doing should be modified or avoided. Forcing a child into a boring or painful activity will merely teach the child that the activity is boring and painful, no matter how good we think it is for the child. Anything with a grade should be avoided. Children quickly learn that many school activities are worth doing only for the grade (15).

As teachers then, we should take a different approach to instruction and grades.

(Notice the changes to the left margin, which is double tabbed to begin and then single tabbed through the rest of the borrowed passage; the single spacing; and the absence of quotation marks.)

When citing a website in the written text of the paper, use the sponsor, the organizer, or the designer of the site as the author and whatever page (1, 2, or 3) from which you have taken information. If you are unsure of the author of the site, use the title of the site like this: ("Today's Issues in Health," 3). Later in the paper, abbreviate the title: ("Today's," 4).

(continues)

> **BOX 9.2 (*continued*)**
>
> To set up the works cited page use the author or; if there is no author, use the article title in alphabetical order. Once you've listed all the authors and article titles in alphabetical order, do the websites in alphabetical order if the sites have no sponsors or organizations to use as authors. Sample website citation:
>
> > Author(s), "Article Title," date (Web address).
>
> Always underline the title of the book, movie, or magazine and put article titles in quotation marks.
>
> Do not use pronouns in the formal sections of the paper—the statement of the problem and the review of the literature.
>
> Also, use twelve-point, double-spaced, Times Roman font.
>
> Write out numbers of one or two words (e.g., fifty-three) unless you will use many numbers and percentages; then use numerals consistently throughout the paper.

though is set up so that failing the review of literature section dooms the writer to a low grade.

The conclusion of the paper is easy to write. Students review the statement of the problem and then consider what they've concluded based on their research. From there they craft their own ending, which need not be more than a page or two. Finally, they develop a selected bibliography, based on a sample that was photocopied from a model student paper and distributed to the class prior to the activity. So, putting all the parts together is just a matter of organization.

Grading

The overall assignment sheet (Box 9.3) explains how the paper will be graded and why.

BOX 9.3
Research Paper for Grade 11 English

1. Your paper must contain the following:

   - title page with your name, homeroom, English class period, date, teacher's name, and title of your paper.
   - table of contents page.
   - introduction—one-page explanation of why you chose to write and research this topic.
   - statement of the problem—a description of the issue you will address, why it is important, and what you hope to prove or learn. This section will also be one or two pages in length. Essentially, this is your *thesis* statement.
   - review of the literature—an analysis of what you learned from the *ten sources of information* you read. This is the main body of your paper and should be four to seven pages long.
   - summary and conclusion—what you have learned from your research and how it supported or changed your thesis (this section should be from one to three pages in length).
   - works cited page.

2. Schedule of *due dates* for paper sections to be submitted in class:

   - 2/17–2/21, topic of paper submitted to instructor
   - 2/24–2/25, statement of problem (peer edit)
   - 3/4–3/5, list of references (ten sources are required)
   - 3/13–3/14, outline of review of literature (to be peer-edited in class)
   - 3/20–3/21, first draft of review of literature.
   - 3/26–3/27, completed and revised review of literature
   - 4/2–4/3, summary and conclusion (peer edit)
   - 4/9–4/10, final copy of paper with works cited page submitted for final grade

(continues)

BOX 9.3 (continued)

Note: Much of your work on this paper will be in the form of drafts done and edited in class. If you have your section of the paper ready on the day listed, you will benefit from the help of others. *If your section is late, you run the risk of trying to turn in a paper of high quality without the support and advice of your teacher and classmates.* Each section will be graded as 100, 95, 90, 60, or 0, and you will receive a 60 (F) for class work every day your section is late. The class work grade is factored into the quarter grade. A grading rubric will be given to you.

GRADING RUBRIC/RESEARCH PAPER/ENGLISH 11

A++ (100)—exceeds standard with honors
Each paper segment has no errors in spelling, grammar, or section format. Assignment is typed as neatly as possible; has factual evidence from primary sources to support opinion; is thoughtful, detailed, and well-written; and displays an extraordinary attempt to be as well done—and thoroughly done—as possible. Great care by the writer to create an exceptional response is obvious.

A+ (95)—exceeds standard
Same as above; no obvious errors exist in paper's presentation (grammar spelling, format) or response (no lack of reference or source evidence). A minor error or two may be evident, but overall the paper is well done and competently written. Writing may not be as well thought out or as thorough as in A++ response.

A (90)—meets standard
Same as above; some minor errors are present, but paper is well written and meets the criteria for a properly done assignment. Response may also have been a revision of a paper that received a lower grade. *This grade is the expected result of your effort.* Any paper and/or section failing to meet this grade must be revised before the final due date.

> F (60)—below standard
> Obvious errors requiring a rewrite exist. The requirement is a revision to an A grade.
>
> 0—No reasonable attempt was ever made to complete the paper.
>
> *Note:* Aside from having no obvious errors, a *well-written* paper is logical and easy to read; has few passive-voice sentences and no run-on sentences or fragments; has all quotes or paraphrased passages properly cited (MLA); is paragraphed correctly; and doesn't mix verb tenses. Having your paper section ready on each due date for your classmates and teacher to review will give you the opportunity to have a paper that meets the standard for the course. In addition, students unprepared for the due dates receive an F (60) every day their paper section is late, and this is factored in to the quarter grade. *This paper represents the major part of your third- and fourth-quarter grades and is the primary focus of your class work.*

Each section earns A, F, or 0 grades, to be consistent with the workshop process, but emphasis is placed on having each section in on time. The student earns an A grade for each written section—provided each is revised as necessary—and A grades for meeting deadlines; an F grade is given for each day past the due date. In effect, a student can earn an A grade for the paper but have an F grade for missing deadlines, which when averaged together is a low passing grade.

Emphasizing timeliness is critical to the overall momentum of the process, and poor grades for failure to meet due dates should be given out early and often; in fact, other than simply not doing the assignment, being excessively tardy with work is the only way to fail. An F is carried in the grade book for every day that a section is late, which amounts to points lost.

Since each section is weighed differently in the grade book, the points lost can add up, but it is important to remember that the writing of the paper is one grade and the timeliness of its completion is another. Having "points-off" penalties will eventually make not writing the paper the better option. Why bother to write it at all when the best grade is an F?

By establishing a writing grade separate from an effort (meeting deadline) grade, the paper is still worth writing, the effort grade stands, and it—rather than strictly the paper—is factored into the overall quarter grade. Also, because the format of the paper is easier to manage and the student is writing about a topic of interest with lots of peer and teacher input, it is rare to have someone not do it.

Another way to use grades to motivate is to begin the paper in the third quarter. At some point, a paper section deadline will fall near the end of the quarter, and one can reward those students who work ahead of deadline by counting twice a grade for being timely.

For example, if the first draft of the review of literature is due a few days before the end of a quarter, there will be some pupils who miss the due date and earn Fs for class work. Those who do meet the deadline earn A grades. The teacher can then carry over the grade into the next marking period until all first drafts are in, so those who have worked ahead of the others get extra credit.

In effect, a grade for the review of literature finished in the third quarter is added again into the fourth so a student has an A in both quarterly columns. Adding the class work grade to both quarters rewards those who work diligently. Motivated students appreciate carrying over the grade since their effort is supported and recognized, and work ethic is developed as a class expectation.

Another motivator is the fact that this is a paper format that they can use in the future as a model, so taking the time to do it right can pay dividends in the long run. It is important for students to realize that by writing the paper to the expected proficiency of an A grade, they've made a competent model of their own to follow.

Since first-time users of the Skinner method can have problems with it, remember that the paper stands alone as its own grade and that class work provides another grade. Here's how to set up a class work grade:

If the student works within reason, her grade for the day is an A or 90. If she has to be reminded more than once to get busy or she missed a deadline, her grade is an F, which is considered a 60. If she refused to work, disrupted others or the class, she was sent out of the room and earned a 0. In this way, effort is as important as the quality of what is produced. At the end of the quarter, a student could have 90 for the entire paper and 60 for class work, so the quarter grade would be 75. This is a simple example, but keeping grades simple is also a good motivator.

After a while, some students complain that the highest grade they can earn is an A, which is nonsense. If a section of the paper is done exceptionally well the first time or a student works ahead of deadline, in both instances a 100 grade is recorded and factored into the quarter's average. What's amazing about the "I can only earn a 90 grade" whine is that when one traditionally grades writing and never uses the workshop approach, very few students earn exceptional grades.

In the traditional English class, the grading scheme one uses is essentially based on a moving target, meaning that more often than not one establishes a class grade based on the best paper and then works backwards, or down, on the grade scale. With the Skinner approach, the level of quality is constant, much more excellent work is done, and students earn higher grades, yet they still complain—but this is not a surprise to those who have worked for any time with adolescents.

CHAPTER TEN
PORTFOLIOS, ASSESSMENT, AND METACOGNITION

Excellent assessment shapes students' thinking and learning in ways that allow them to have control and understanding over their skills and abilities. It should help them avoid error, revise, write and read purposefully, make connections, and analyze and solve problems based on the good learner habits they develop. Excellent assessment is about supporting and sometimes accelerating growth for each student. It is not simply about grading an end product; rather, it is an involved, everyday process. For this to happen, we need to have an understanding of what is involved in good teaching, learning, thinking, evaluating, and producing in the class.

Chapter 7 included a discussion using the teaching of literature to create looped thinking from one's writing to one's reading.

The building of student reading and writing folders (or in-progress or formative portfolios), the development of Writers' Notebooks (WNBs), and the use of literature circles and peer-editing allow a teacher to not only design authentic lessons (those based on the demonstrated strengths and weaknesses of the students in the class) but to set learning goals based on measurement of real thinking.

PORTFOLIOS, ASSESSMENT, AND METACOGNITION

Norman L. Webb's "Depth of Knowledge" hierarchy defines four levels of thinking that expand well beyond assessing what one might consider to be surface learning, more commonly known as regurgitated learning or tests and quizzes. Some of Webb's Level 3 writing performance indicators are the following:

- Support ideas with details and examples.
- Use voice appropriate to the purpose and audience.
- Edit writing to produce logical progression of ideas.

Level 4 expects that students will "write an analysis of two selections, identifying the common theme and generating a purpose that is appropriate for both."

Webb, based on Karen Wixson and E. Dutro's 1999 research relating to primary-grade reading standards, defines these Level 3 thinking goals for readers:

- Determine the author's purpose and describe how it affects the interpretation of the reading selection.
- Summarize information from multiple sources to address a specific topic.
- Analyze and describe the characteristics of various types of literature.

Level 4 thinking includes the following:

- Analyze and synthesize information.
- Examine and explain alternative perspectives across a variety of sources.
- Describe and illustrate how common themes are found across texts from different cultures.

CHAPTER TEN

(In fairness to Webb, there's more defined in his Depth of Knowledge schema and it is certainly worth reading. The selected skills here are easily demonstrated and mastered in a workshop class.) Here one would add the qualifier to Webb's hierarchy: Students should meet all these performance indicators *correctly*.

To complete these thinking activities, a number of conditions must exist. Students must see the value in doing Level 3 and 4 thinking. It must matter to them in a demonstrable way.

None of the levels here are impossible, but it's the degree to which they are done that matters, and that requires students who are willing to work, based on the measurable growth they perceive in learning. They must be aware of what they will be asked to study and see the reasons why; they must have attainable goals that they help write with the teacher early in the school year; and they must replicate the habits of learning as defined by Robert Marzano in his book, *A Different Kind of Classroom: Teaching with the Dimensions of Learning*.

Marzano identifies the "Habits of Mind" that all successful adults have, from the simple, such as being on time and persevering, to the difficult, such as the ability and willingness to think about one's thinking, or to engage in metacognition.

Marzano and Webb provide an additional overlay for assessment that includes the following in a workshop class: self-motivation, determination, self-reflection, productive student habits, respect for others, love of learning, and, of course, all that they are required to learn in regard to literacy—a good bit to accomplish for sure. So the question is how to use assessment to build and reinforce these habits and skills, and that's where portfolio building with a purpose from the first school day to the last becomes essential.

Defining goals begins with a sense of where the class is in terms of what they think they know about Language Arts. Beginning the year with some reflective questions can help focus the group on where they are and where you will need to lead them. A good way to start is to have them write answers to the following questions:

- Are you a reader? If so, what do you like about reading, and what do you read?

- Do you write poems, stories, or songs? Do you feel you write well?

- What does someone have to do to succeed in an English class?

- What do you think you will do well this year in this class?

- What will you need help with in English this year?

- What did you like about last year's English class? Did you have a good year?

- How can I help you read, write, and think better in this class?

Of course, some of the answers to these questions will be less than stimulating, but the poor responses are always an indicator of a student's confidence and attitude in the subject.

The Language Arts Self-Assessment sheet (Box 5.11) is more specific and gives a focus to the skills and habits that will be needed, learned, and expected to be successful. Also, once the Listener's Checklist and Peer-Editing sheets are introduced, the class will have a purposeful, overall focus, and all that is left to do early in the year is to bring those goals to the forefront.

The Personal Literacy Goals (Box 5.12) center around four critical areas of instruction: reading and writing fluency, critical self-awareness, critical awareness of others, and awareness of academic expectations. Using newspaper-print sheets posted on the classroom walls, students brainstorm, list, and discuss suggestions under each heading to formulate bullets for each one. Some suggestions are simple, "I need to spell better"; others are more difficult like, "I can't picture a story when I read." Others have to do with habit: "I need to concentrate," while some relate to effort, "I have to finish what I start." Eventually the teacher rewords, "Understand how a story works to figure out the ideas better," to "I can read like a writer" and explains to them that this is the thinking of an expert—in this case Frank Smith—that they've suggested as a goal.

It gets students' attention when the instructor points out that they have basically fallen in line with a scholar on reading and writing.

It takes a week or so to finalize the list, and there is really no rush—the longer these ideas are "out there," the more they set the tone for the workshop. Over time, the list is agreed upon, finished, and added to their folders. This activity empowers students because they have a hand in what will matter to them, establishes a critical thinking context, and sets an essential tone relating to the habits of successful learners.

At this point, an overriding purposefulness for the school year is established and everything to be done is linked and referred to again and again as the year moves along. Nothing is taught, done, or planned that isn't part of a larger context, whether it is writing better or just learning how to speak meaningfully, thoughtfully, and considerately about the work of the class. As a result, every day matters, and how one works through the class each day not only shapes one's skills, but also one's habits and attitudes.

Once the yearlong context is established and the students have a sense of expectation, the next step is to document progress toward those goals with an end-of-the-year, or summative, portfolio. Works to be included represent that which is dictated by the district curriculum and National Performance Standards in English Language Arts (ELA). (How one would determine any of this, including which personal literacy goals should be emphasized for a class, is entirely up to the teacher. What is provided here is only a starting point.)

Just as with any graded class activity, the portfolio grade will also have parameters that have to be met (Box 8.3). The grading scheme expects all work to be of an A level of quality at minimum. The final portfolio requirements are the first assignments that the class reviews immediately after the midyear break and are the primary activities for the remainder of the year.

Once these goals are in place, the workshop class becomes a connected learning community that has many goals for the success of students and is based on metacognition, the development of good learning habits, and best practice strategies that are documented as being the best way to teach all students. All that is left for the teacher then is to make sure the process remains undisturbed, that the class routine for success and the building of portfolios stays on track, and that the students are monitored toward the meeting of these goals through conferences and informal dialogue.

The status-of-the-class notation, portfolios (formative and summative), goals and self-assessment sheets, the workshop style of the class, and many opportunities to discuss reading and writing with peers and the teacher together create an assessment momentum of its own that moves the class purposefully from day to day.

Finally, an outline of those assignments done in class over the course of the year and what ELA performance standards they meet (Box 10.1), helps students chart their progress toward learning and sets the class up as standards-based.

With all the information presented to students regarding learner expectations, goals, models of work, and clear rubrics, students can answer questions relating to what they are learning and why, how their work meets the performance standards for the discipline, what progress they have made toward those expectations, and what to do to improve upon their work; these are the hallmarks of a standards-based methodology driven by best practice.

CHAPTER TEN

> ## BOX 10.1
> ### Performance Standards/Language Arts in Practice
>
> #### E-1/READING:
>
> Read twenty-five books.
> *Action—self-directed reading, literature circles, summer reading.*
>
> Form opinions about stories, poems, or literature based on how well they are written.
> *Action—book summary and book evaluation essays, WNB.*
>
> Read a book and retell or write a short explanation to describe it (summarize).
> *Action—book summary essay, double entry journal.*
>
> Read two or more books, poems, story excerpts, or articles and decide what's the same and what's different about them.
> *Action—compare and contrast essay.*
>
> Understand the difference between writing creatively and writing for academic, classroom purposes.
> *Action—writing workshop assignments ("two pages"), essays written about novel or autobiographical excerpts.*
>
> Understand the author's theme or main idea.
> *Action—Go Ask Alice and book evaluation essays, author's theme project.*
>
> Organize and gather information to support an opinion.
> *Action—book summary, book evaluation, and compare and contrast essays, basic essay format assignments.*
>
> Knowing how a writer's style and use of words can keep the reader interested.
> *Action—book evaluation essay, Listener's Checklist.*

Understanding how authors add many ideas to their writing by use of unique detail, special character traits, exact setting, symbols (the heart symbolically represents love), irony (the opposite of what you'd expect), foreshadowing (giving the reader the sense that something bad will happen), and plot twists.

Action—*observation writing in WNB, short answer essays from novel, poetry, and autobiographical excerpts.*

E-2/WRITING:

Narrative essay (telling the reader of an event) and creative writing to keep the reader interested.

Action—*midterm exam, Listener's and Writer's Checklist, "two page" writing assignments, observations assignments in WNB.*

Writing a persuasive essay (make reader agree with your opinion) and a reflective essay (think about and explain your actions).

Action—*book summary, book evaluation, compare and contrast and final exam essays, basic essay format, final exam, WNB.*

E-3/CONFERENCING:

Review of work with classmates and teacher.

Action—*recording of pages read daily in class (teacher), Skills Sheet, Listener's and Writer's Edit Sheets, Second Term Assignment Checklist, Final Portfolio Checklist.*

Use positive comments to evaluate the work of others, and encourage others to revise and improve their writing.

Action—*Listener's and Writer's Checklist, Writers' Carousel, Author's Chair, Skills Sheet, "By now you will be . . ." list, A—F—0 grades for all papers and assignments.*

CHAPTER ELEVEN
STARTING THE SCHOOL YEAR IN THE WORKSHOP MODEL

Now that the workshop class has been laid out, it is time to look at the actual planning from day to day.

Day One

After getting the names, addresses, and parent contacts, students take home letters for parents to sign that explain the class and the grading scheme (Box 11.1). Because there are no books like one would expect (grammar, spelling, or literature), parents will wonder about the class unless a letter is sent home. Having it signed and returned is important in the event that a parent later has a concern with the instructional methodology. The signed letter provides the teacher with documentation from the first week of school of the parent's acknowledgment of the change of teaching approach.

It may not seem like much, but it is important for administrators to know that this is made clear to parents from the beginning; this allows the administrators to stand fully behind the instructor if a misunderstanding were to arise. Over the years many teachers have earned nothing but praise for a workshop class, but it is wise to make parents aware from the beginning.

BOX 11.1

Date

High School

Street or Avenue

City, State

Phone Number

Dear Parent/Guardian:

    I would like you to know what you can expect from your son's/daughter's grade 11 American literature class this year.

    For the most part, all students work independently on different reading and writing projects as part of a final, graded portfolio. As a result, you can plan on your son or daughter doing the following:

- Four pages of creative writing and five half to full pages of private journal/Writer's Notebook writing in and out of class per week
- Fifty to one hundred pages of reading with two pages of writing related to it
- Multiple American literature reading and study packets done in relation to the reading anthology—these are the main reading requirements for the course
- A research paper (date / topic to be determined).

In addition, since this is the minimum required, you can insist that your son or daughter do more for extra credit—something I strongly encourage—at any time, all semester long. (For example, do eight pages of creative writing a week.) A grade scale for writing and classwork is on the back.

    If you have any questions, please call.

Thank you,

Teacher Name
(Please sign and return.)

x _____

(This form letter is copied on school stationary before it is given out to students.)

CHAPTER ELEVEN

After passing out the letter and reading the part to the students that explains the class, an informal survey, such as the one suggested in chapter 10 regarding their attitudes toward ELA, is done. Finally, they are asked to bring in a book of their own for the next class and a notebook. It is explained that we will begin each class with a writing entry and then move on to reading a book of their own.

Day Two

The teacher explains the placement of personal entries into the Writer's Notebook (WNB), including that students are to divide it into two sections and work toward the middle. The front is used for the daily journal entries they will make, while they will begin from the last page and work back as they place any questions, comments, observations, class notes, or other school-related work.

Some reluctant writers don't have a notebook, so they are given an exam "blue book" to begin with; they actually like using them so much that one should keep a healthy supply of them in class. The students who had never written much are pleased that within a month's time or so they've filled all its pages.

Once we've written, then it's time for students to begin reading quietly from a book of their choosing, or they can quietly come up and select a book from the classroom library. It costs about three hundred dollars to initially stock about five copies of each of the following for grades eight and up: *They Cage the Animals at Night* (Burch), *Hatchet* and *Nightjohn* (Paulsen), *The Cage* (Sender), *The Contender* (Lipstye), *It Happened to Nancy* and *Go Ask Alice* (Anonymous/Sparks), *Sarah T.: Portrait of a Teenage Alcoholic* (Wagner), and *A Child Called "It"* (Pelzer), among others that students will read.

Having five copies of high-interest books on hand is necessary so that if a few students are reading them, they can organize themselves into groups for book discussions.

Another reason for multiple copies is that if a student came in raving about a book, others would want to read it; the teacher can build off their enthusiasm by having other copies handy.

After twenty minutes, ask students to flip to the back of their WNBs, write down the date, and make a prediction about the story for the next reading.

Since the pages read are recorded daily, the teacher can give the reluctant readers—or any other student for that matter—an A for extra credit if they have doubled the number of pages read before the next day's meeting. The A, when calculated, is about 20 percent of a point, but they don't know that, and it feels great to earn an A, especially for the reluctant reader.

Give extra credit too for opening and writing a journal entry before the class begins. When walking into the room, note who is writing without being asked, and also give out As to them. It is nice to be able to say, "Please close your journals now and take out your book. Today, everyone earned an A."

Awarding extra credit, rather than using grades to support failure, fosters a positive climate and creates good learner habits. (Traditionally, grading operates on a deficit model that the student has little control over, is highly arbitrary—who hasn't given a point or two to a student that wasn't solely based on learned achievement?—and is focused on what was done wrong rather than on what was done right: How many times has it been said to a student, "Gee, if it weren't for one little mistake right there, you'd have had an 87"? This minimizes the overall grade and diffuses student effort.)

After five minutes of quiet journal entries and twenty of reading, students are given manila folders that will eventually contain all their creative work. Obviously with this routine a pattern or "quiet strategy" for classroom management emerges.

Students need to think and read without distraction. So many times reading fails because the teacher, rather than reading with the class, is conferencing with a pupil or talking out in the hall with another colleague. Distraction breaks the spell of a quiet strategy and must be avoided. The class will move from quiet reading to fifteen minutes of quiet writing, then they can ask permission to peer-edit or conference.

Setting up the writing folder requires that name, homeroom, and class period be written on the manila tab so that the folders can be kept in a file drawer in the class. Students staple into the folder the rules for Writing Days. Then the first rule—You are free to write about whatever you want—is explained to mean that *tastefully* they can write poems, songs, raps, stories, or whatever else they'd like. Right away, a good lesson about audience is necessary, just as it is needed for the journal entries.

Notebooks should not contain information that would embarrass the teacher, school, or its students, and no unattended notebook should ever be open or read—lessons of decency and privacy that really hit home as the journal is filled.

Day Three

After journal entries and self-directed reading, an observation assignment starts the writing process well. A trip to the library, gym, a busy hallway, or an outside area jumpstarts the activity.

Upon returning to class, students should be asked to list the words in their written observations that show action, color, sound, smell, time, or feel and any other words or phrases that they feel are interesting or well done. At home, they are to revise the passage as well as they can with the intention of reading it to classmates, and they should be prepared to explain why they made the changes they did.

An observation assignment is a great way for students and the instructor to get to know one another. What the pupil writes about, what she chooses to revise, and what she observes provide valuable insight into her likes, interests, and attitude—key indicators for classroom planning and individual student success—that would take a long time to learn in other ways.

Day Four

Again, class begins with journal entry and self-directed reading, then the students break into groups of three and four to read and review the observation assignment. They are to tell about the original written version, then discuss what they changed and why. Finally, they are to read the revision and ask for reactions. Students give feedback based on what they liked and if there were any similarities to their own writing.

The groups eventually report out to the class with someone recording the comments on the board or overhead. Looking for similar themes, ideas, or concerns is important as it brings the group together and lets them see that what writers do, generally, is the same: They struggle, wonder, change, discard, and redo.

Closing the lesson involves a final revision that should take into account what was discussed in the group and class and how a written piece can be made better. For example, feedback that suggested more about an aspect of the observation should be incorporated into a final draft. At home, students revise; they are told that they will be tested on the assignment the next day.

Day Five

After following the same opening class routine, students are given this task, which is their first "test":

Look over the drafts of your observation assignment and answer these questions as specifically as possible:

- What part of your observation did you choose to revise and why? What was the result?

- What was learned from the discussion of your work and did it impact your revision of it?

- What did hearing the writing of your classmates, and their comments, help you learn about writing or about yourself?

CHAPTER ELEVEN

- If we were to do another observation assignment, would you take a different approach?

Have students turn in responses along with all the drafts of their observation when finished. (One could choose to collect the whole notebook, but ripping the assignment out, putting names and page numbers on all sheets, and then stapling them together for the writing folder is a better option.)

With a simple observation assignment, and right from the first few days of classes, students are rereading, writing, and thinking critically and analytically about literacy. No traditional lesson that was ever done before brings a class to life so purposefully, intensely, and enthusiastically in so short a time.

Days Six through Ten

The routine of the class is established and it is time to solidify the writing workshop format. If a class is dominated by reluctant writers, the plan is to make lists of topics about which to write, describe how to flesh those topics out, and move to first drafts. The grading of the class requires that every other day or so a student can show writing or the attempt to write, which earns an A.

Focus lessons should begin by explaining the Listener's Checklist, how it is to be filled out, and how it is to be used as part of a revision. During days seven to ten different parts of the Peer-Edit Sheet are used as lessons on basic grammar and the class process for revision. As always, keeping grammar and mechanics simple to understand makes the editing process go smoothly. Proper paragraphing is better explained in this handout than in any grammar book lesson (Box 11.2).

After two weeks the class routine should be established, and students who have finished their books should be ready to write book summaries or book evaluations, depending upon their ability level.

BOX 11.2
Guidelines for Starting New Paragraphs

You must start a new paragraph for the following:

1. *A new speaker.* When a new character speaks in your story, start a new paragraph.

   Example from *Nightjohn* by Gary Paulsen (52),

   > "Bee," he said. "It be B."
   > "That sounds crazy...." (Sarney said.)
   > "That's how you say the letter. B. It's for beh or be or buh or boo. That's how a B looks and how you make the sound."

2. *A new time.* When time changes in your story, start a new paragraph.

   Example from *Waiting* by Ha Jin (77),

   > He left a widow and three small children. His death disturbed Manna profoundly, as she had known him by sight.
   > The next evening when they were walking on the fringe of the sports ground, she sighed and said to Lin, "Life is such a precarious thing."

3. *A new place.* When action moves to a new place, start a new paragraph.

   Example from *Whale Pirates* by Dennis Kafalas (53),

   > Billy put the binoculars up to his eyes. Arrow was sitting at a table looking at the contents of a gray, steel security box, while the cat sat in his lap. Billy amused himself with the notion that maybe the old sailor was looking at a treasure map.
   > Billy crawled closer to the house, hoping to get a better view. He moved to a spot near a small garden behind the cabin.

4. *A new idea.* When you write a new idea into your story, start a new paragraph.

(continues)

CHAPTER ELEVEN

> **BOX 11.2 (continued)**
>
> Example from *Go Ask Alice*, Anonymous (14),
>
> > Sorry I haven't had time to write for two days, but we haven't stopped. We're still trying to get curtains hung and boxes unpacked and things put away. The house is beautiful. The walls are thick dark wood and there are two steps going down into a long sunken living room....
> >
> > I'm still worried about school and TODAY I must go. I wish Tim were in high school. Even a little brother would be better than no one, but he is in his second year of junior high.
>
> *A "rule of thumb": You should have about three paragraphs per written page.

With middle schoolers or struggling readers, they should also keep a reading journal, which aids comprehension enormously.

Ask them, between pages thirty to fifty, to write from the perspective of the main character. It need only be a half-page to full-page entry, and it need only be done at thirty- to fifty-page intervals. Questions to consider might be the following: Pretend you are the main character. What is important to you? What makes you happy or sad? What is your life like and what do you think will happen in the future? These types of questions connect text to self, which is an important reading strategy.

Later, when a student finishes a book, conference with them; scan their journals quickly; give an A, A+, or A++ (90, 95, or 100), depending on the effort and quality evident in their work; and be pleased to find that one can learn much about what reading skills they possess. Something in the books they have read will always jump out, and a discussion leading to deeper thinking about the novels will follow.

Sometimes the "reality" of the story is questioned and teacher and student can look specifically at the passage that created the issue. Reviewing it leads to conversations about what is "wrong" with the writing of it, how it could have been more realistic, and how this can translate to better writing in general—a lesson that should also be shared with the class.

Again, this type of dialogue based upon a trade book, as opposed to a textbook, is more meaningful and likely to be better remembered than any artificial lesson from an anthology.

Any questions related to reading should always attempt to create meaning through text-to-text, text-to-self, and text-to-world connections and through strategies that help students create mental images in their minds. These strategies are further explained in *Mosaic of Thought: Teaching Comprehension in a Reader's Workshop* (by E. Keene and S. Zimmerman), *When Kids Can't Read* (by K. Beers), and *Literature Circles: Voice and Choice in Book Clubs and Reading Groups* (by H. Daniels), all of which are worth adding to one's professional collection.

Depending on the grade and level taught, the reading journal, book summary, or book evaluation should result from the complete reading of the student-selected texts. If the book evaluation is an appropriate starting point for the class, focus lessons on the standards to evaluate a book should be done since they link the reading of fiction to the writing of it, which imbeds thinking about fiction in both the reading and writing workshop.

If the evaluation is the starting point, then less time is needed to explain the workshop process or how to use the checklist and peer-editing sheet, so more time can be devoted to explaining the book standards, which came from William Appel and Denise Sterr's book, *The Truth about Fiction (Writing)*.

Grades

After two weeks, there will be a daily journal and reading grade, a writing workshop Two-Page grade, the observation assignment test, and possibly a book summary. Grades are A++ (100), A+ (95),

CHAPTER ELEVEN

A (90), F (60), and 0. Below are the grades of four students, without a grade higher than A and with no extra credit. The reason no other grades are considered is that, at this point, a baseline for assignments and scores for A and F have to be determined first, then the actual numerical value of each A, F, or 0 can be assigned. So let's look at Lisa's grades. She has all As and can help determine the baseline sum.

Lisa

Reading/daily WNB journal: (week 1) A, A, A, A, A; (week 2) A, A, A, A, A
Writing: A, A (from Two-Page assignment)
Book Summary: 5 As (required revision until A was earned)
Observation Assignment test: 5 As
Overall grade (from 22 total): A or 90 (22 × 90 = 1,980 ÷ 90 = 90).

Milhouse

Reading/daily WNB journal: (week 1) A, A, A, A, A; (week 2) A, A, A, A, A
Writing: A, F (from Two-Page assignment)
Book Summary: 5 As (required revision until A was earned),
Observation Assignment test: 5 As
Overall grade: A or 90 (21 × 90 = 1,890 + 60 = 1,950 ÷ 22 = 88.6 or 89).

Martin

Reading/daily WNB journal: (week 1) F, F, F, F, F; (week 2) F, F, F, F, F
Writing: F, F (from Two-Page assignment)
Book Summary: 5 Fs (no revision until A was earned)
Observation Assignment test: 5 Fs (no revision)
Overall grade: F or 60 (22 × 60 = 1,320 ÷ 22 = 60).

STARTING THE SCHOOL YEAR IN THE WORKSHOP MODEL

Bart

Reading/daily WNB journal: (week 1) F, F, F, F, F; (week 2) F, F, F, F, F
Writing: F, F (from Two-Page assignment)
Book Summary: 0 (refused to even attempt)
Observation Assignment test: 5 Fs (revision not done)
Overall grade: 46 (17 × 60 = 1,020 ÷ 22 = 46).

From these four categories we can determine that over the two weeks, and based on the number of grades recorded, a sum for a 90 was based on twenty-two possible grades, and every F score diminished the 90 grade by 1.4 points. To check, 1.4 multiplied by 22 is 30.8. If you add 30.8 to the score of 60 (all Fs), the total is 90.8 or 91.

Also, using twenty-two grades as a base, a 0 score takes 4.1 points off (21 × 90 = 1,890 + 0 ÷ 22 = 85.9 or 86). To check, all 0s would be: 4.1 × 22 = 90.2, so the 4.1 value for a 0 is correct.

Establishing a scale with an A, F, or 0 means that all grades will fall between 60 and 90, and it's just a matter of determining what one A is worth.

To find the value of an A grade, add up all the possible assignments, multiply the sum by 90, then factor in one 60 grade in place of a 90. For example, thirty A grades would equal a sum of 2,700 (90 × 30). Twenty-nine A grades would equal 2,610. With one F grade, the total for thirty grades is 2,670 (2,610 + 60). In this case, every F grade subtracts one point from 90 (2,670 ÷ 30 = 89).

A student with fifteen As and fifteen Fs has a 75 average because 15 points were lost. Using the same baseline of thirty grades, a student with twenty-nine As and one 0 would have an 86.6 or 87 (2,610 ÷ 30 = 87). Roughly every 0 would reduce the 90 score by three points.

Once the values for an F and 0 are determined, it's just a matter of scanning grade columns and subtracting the Fs, or zeroes if any, from 90. Over time, it's easier than using a computer.

CHAPTER ELEVEN

Once the range from 90 to 60 is determined, students who score higher than an A must be factored as well by using the same process. Again, thirty A grades equal 2,700. If one of those grades is a 95, then the total will be 2,705. Every 95 grade adds a tenth of a point (2,705 ÷ 30 is 90.1). If there is a 100 score, the sum is 2,710 ([(30 × 90) + 10] or [(29 × 90) + 100]). Every 100 (A++) adds 0.3 (2,710 ÷ 30 = 90.3). So a student with three A+ grades and two A++ scores adds 0.3 and 0.6 to the total (0.9) for a 91 grade (90 + 0.9).

Finally, there's extra credit, which is simply worth 0.2, based on a five-day-a-week meeting schedule. This score was determined without any mathematical foundation; it was first used primarily to motivate students to open their WNBs without being asked.

Extra credit was used daily to create good classroom and student habits, hence the 0.2 point determination. After forty-five days in a quarter, a student could have as many as 8 (45 × 0.2) points extra credit. The obvious thought is that the class will earn quite a few 90-plus grades and a couple 100s. Yes, but think about what the grades represent.

Every student who earned above 90 was reading, writing, revising, thinking, and doing quality work that embodied all the essential skills and concepts that needed to be learned and understood on a daily basis. These same students were self-motivated, set good examples for others, and had the habits of successful learners. Was a class like this deserving of 90-plus grades? No doubt. Would they score well on a fifty-question grammar quiz? Not necessarily, but what mattered more?

Over the course of the semester these students became literate, and like the literate, didn't need to know every rule of grammar to read and write effectively. Looking at the final portfolios proved beyond a doubt that the grades were justified and that the gifted of the group had earned higher grades, much as they would have with a traditional scale.

The final portfolios also demonstrated more than any conventional grading could, showing how meaningful goals were met and became part of a student's manner of thinking and learning.

However one decides to grade, it is important to remember that this scale rewards not only product, but effort, thinking, and learner habits more than any other system. Although the A, F, 0 scale may take some getting used to, it is worth trying a scoring method that motivates and encourages as this one does and one that, once it's understood, makes grading easy for both teacher and student. It becomes a running record that can be referred to every day.

Many reluctant students love looking at their grades. The As and Fs listed by their names gives them a sense of their daily progress; they don't have to wait until the middle of the quarter to know where they stand.

Two Weeks and Beyond

It is important to remember that the workshop is the basis for class instruction and that the model—and its quiet thinking strategies—is to remain in place. If too many interruptions occur, especially with reluctant learners, then the gains in habit and routine that allow for literacy growth are broken up.

With some classes the routine can vary occasionally since students who read and write fairly well quickly internalize the thinking strategies to improve, but with those whose literacy is just emerging, the routine is to be reinforced daily well into the year. What is forgotten sometimes is that the ELA skills being developed require thinking of the highest order by all students, even if the work they produce isn't always the best. The lower the level of literacy, the more the focus needs to be on developing reading and writing fluency before any meaningful skill development can be learned.

In the long term, it is just a matter of determining where to begin: whether by a reading journal, book summary, or book evaluation as a starting point for academic writing. If the reading journal is not needed, then the plan for academic writing might be two book summaries, two book evaluations, and two compare-and-contrast essays done in relation to self-selected text reading for the year.

CHAPTER ELEVEN

Students should do two of each to reinforce the skills in each one and to ensure that they can move on successfully to the next. These essays serve as the academic writing base of the class, but other essay opportunities and assignments are sprinkled in, depending upon the course.

Usually, the second compare-and-contrast essay needs to be done during the fourth quarter. Some students will struggle while others will be ahead of the game and may be ready to tackle an "author's theme" essay created from the *Go Ask Alice* passage described in Box 5.5. What is obvious over the long term is that some work faster and better than others, but the beauty is that those who can are not held back as they would be in a traditional, teacher-directed class. They set their own pace and establish a great work ethic for others.

In terms of writing, a number of grammar issues will become evident, like when and how to use quotes from text—among others—and that can be a lesson. By being alert to the issues that develop within the class, one can plan meaningful lessons that advance reading, writing, and thinking.

No matter what the level of ability or age, though, always review the basic essay format because students need to understand that the essay is designed to suit their writing purposes, and it is as expandable and flexible as they need it to be to successfully transfer their thoughts.

Over the course of the year, it is referred to on many occasions from the argumentative essay to, if need be, the research paper. Students see the format fitting their purposes as a writer, as opposed to the other way around, where they try to negotiate a five-paragraph scheme and essentially give more thought to how to please the teacher and not to how to best use a formal structure to express their thoughts.

Using the essay structure to suit one's ideas, as opposed to being enslaved by it, is a major difference in thinking, planning, and writing.

The basic essay format also brings deeper understanding to the writing models used to write the summaries and evaluations. Understanding how the models are set up for each type of essay is essential to using them purposefully, and the basic essay format establishes that initial form from which others are then built.

Integrating curricula is the next step for the workshop.

Just as the American literature packets demonstrated, whatever is added has to fit the context of the workshop. It would make no sense to spend five weeks on *The Crucible* if it totally shuts down the workshop, but using parts of *The Crucible* to advance student reading and writing skills and understanding makes sense. It can be pared down to some key scenes that ask students to look at character, plot, irony, or all three.

For example, here are some possible questions: How has Miller created suspense with his characters? What passage or snippets of dialogue makes John Proctor real, believable, or tragic? What writing skill is used to make the main characters seem real and how can we use it in our writing?

When adding curricular elements, it is important to consider the following: How will the teaching of this add to the students' literate abilities? What about this adds to our critical thinking, our habits, our understanding of how to use language purposefully?

If those questions cannot be answered, then either the item is not worth teaching or only parts of it should be taught or folded into the workshop class and the rest scrapped. Memorizing passages of Shakespeare may have some brain training use, but too much of it is useless to our understanding of literature. Knowing all the prepositions is another good brain exercise, but it does not advance one's writing abilities in a meaningful way.

Unfortunately, students are exposed to these lessons far too often, and while reciting the litany of prepositions or a Shakespearean sonnet might make one a hit at a party, these skills are basically useless when becoming sophisticated in literacy.

One should gather materials and plan focus lessons wisely, and not sweat the state tests or departmental gossip: The workshop class is well beyond the scope of textbook-dominated curriculum reinforced by one-dimensional state testing. Workshop teachers teach thinking, habit, and perseverance, and they provide the opportunity to be creative and empowered to learn—can any test successfully measure that? Can any test measure the confidence to succeed that a workshop class instills in its participants?

If one adopts best practice, she'll be ahead of the curve pedagogically and in line with the national movement to improve teaching and learning for all students. Also, the National Writing Project, based in California, has a chapter in each state that can support and sustain personal growth with workshop methodology—don't be shy. Nothing is more rewarding than to be around professionals who are truly invested in the profession.

Finally, two thoughts: first, there is a design to authentic practice (Box 11.3) that can help with lesson planning, and second, grading and assessment are to *encourage* learning; students should feel that they can work on something until they not only get it right or earn a passing grade, but until they truly understand the lesson.

Teachers complain that waiting for all students to truly understand a concept takes too much time, but research shows that the time taken is well worth it.

The posting of student work, establishing models for assignments, reworking and refining, and letting students see what is expected of them is the basis for an inquiry- and standards-based class methodology, which has never been embraced as it should have by the profession. Overall, experience proves that once the students' critical "Others" kick in, they gain speed, and by the end of the year have zoomed ahead of where they would have been if one tried to cover more material through a traditional class structure.

Students who feel they can manipulate the learning environment grow exponentially as learners in a workshop class. It is time to give them a class format that encourages and allows for all students to be motivated and invested in their own learning.

BOX 11.3
Designing Authentic Language Arts Practice

The following is a basic guide for creating an authentic learning environment with items that should help focus on the direction, goals, structure, and planning for the class.

SEMESTER OBJECTIVES/GENERAL

- reading/writing fluency to serve as basis for individual growth and sophistication in reading and writing
- student-generated materials to be primary focus of mini-lessons
- Murray's "The Other Self" will represent growth in writer's abilities
- authentic documents, adherence to learning habits (Marzano, "Habits of Mind"), and lesson mastery to serve as basis for grading
- silent reading and creative writing to be linked to enhance critical thinking skills (and appreciation of fiction)
- lessons/projects will be devised—as often as possible—to allow students to work at own pace and independently
- lessons will build upon one another and connecting "evidence" will be obvious to learner
- examples of exceptional work will be available for students to refer to when attempting assignments
- risk-taking and errors are part of the thinking process
- teacher expectations, goals, and grades are clearly defined
- authentic student reading and writing is the top priority of all planning and teaching objectives—students are to be as meaningfully engaged as possible in the Language Arts
- excerpts of great literature/writing will be made available to students on an as-needed basis

(continues)

BOX 11.3 (continued)

DAILY TEACHING/PLANNING OBJECTIVES
(ALL STUDENTS WILL ...)

- have choice and ownership in reading and writing
- move from first draft to final copy at an acceptable pace
- develop a list of reading/writing strengths and weaknesses
- be expected to revise and work to a high level of competency
- work independently, or cooperatively as is necessary, in class
- be expected to bring materials to class, follow class routine, and expect discipline to be nonconfrontational
- understand that brainstorming—and mistakes—is part of the problem-solving and thinking process
- develop positive attitudes toward reading, writing, and learning
- learn to avoid mistakes and recognize (and replicate) successful learning habits
- create final copies for summative (end-of-year) portfolios
- be expected to share what they've learned with others
- learn that writing creatively and for academic purposes are different
- know basic essay format (three paragraphs) and when to use it
- have opportunities to read, discuss, and evaluate well-crafted contemporary fiction
- share and/or gather knowledge in social setting.

QUESTIONS TO KEEP IN MIND
WHEN PLANNING LESSONS

- What does the class need to know in relation to the work they are generating, or will be asked to generate, in the near future?
- What types of problems are all students having?
- Are there individual students who could explain a concept directly to others?
- What, specifically, do I want to see replicated in the class as a result of this lesson?

- Can this entire lesson be done in less than twenty minutes? If not, where should it be broken up into smaller parts?
- Is this lesson connected to another prior lesson, or is it rooted in the authentic work of the class?
- How do I want to evaluate/grade this lesson?
- What will be the motivation for students to learn and internalize the concept?
- Can I introduce related, high-quality fiction to students based on growth and sophistication of class or of an individual student?
- Are there individual students who are ready to move ahead of the others?
- How can this lesson or instruction tie into student interest?
- Are students engaged, making progress and developing a critical awareness of self and discipline?

*Overall, is pace of class acceptable or are there signs of the class bogging down? (Not engaged? Falling behind? Losing interest?)

TEACHING "HARDWARE"

- writing folders (formative portfolio)
- daily journals
- novels of student choice
- book summary (persuasive essay/basic essay format)
- book evaluation essay (critical essay)
- book standards (links reading and writing)
- classroom library
- computers (for word processing)
- summative portfolios
- class "book" (to showcase student work)
- compare-and-contrast essays,
- author's theme or book link projects
- fiction excerpts/focus on literal conventions in basic essay format

(continues)

> **BOX 11.3 (continued)**
>
> ## ASSESSMENT
>
> - All written work will meet A-grade criteria—few if no errors—otherwise revision is expected until work meets criteria.
> - A running record will be kept of writing strengths and weaknesses (Skills Sheet).
> - Corrected errors and taught concepts are expected to be applied to individual writing and that of others.
> - Students will know in advance what assignments are to be completed by end of term, and it is their responsibility to manage time and produce high-quality work.
> - Teacher expectations are relayed to student by Language Arts Assessment sheet, individual conferences, "By now you will be . . ." sheet, and through opportunities to earn extra credit.
> - The process of evaluating work of others, being prepared and on time for class, working to one's ability, producing quality assignments, and respecting the work and effort of classmates are all part of an A, F, or 0 grading system.

SELECTED BIBLIOGRAPHY

American Experience in Literature: Timeless Voices, Timeless Themes. Upper Saddle River, NJ: Prentice-Hall, 1999.
Anonymous. *Go Ask Alice.* New York: Simon & Schuster, 1998.
Appel, W., and D. Sterrs. *The Truth about Fiction (Writing).* Norwalk, CT: Hastings House, 1997.
Atwell, N. *In the Middle: Writing, Reading, and Learning with Adolescents.* Portsmouth, NH: Heinemann, 1987.
Banks, R. *Cloudsplitter.* New York: HarperCollins, 1998.
Beers, K. *When Kids Can't Read: What Teachers Can Do.* Portsmouth, NH: Heinemann, 2003.
Bomer, R. *Time for Meaning: Crafting Literate Lives in Middle and High School.* Portsmouth, NH: Heinemann, 1995.
Daniels, H. *Literature Circles: Voice and Choice in Book Clubs and Reading Groups.* Portland, ME: Stenhouse, 2002.
Daniels, H., A. Hyde, and S. Zemelman. *Best Practice: New Standards for Teaching and Leaning in America's Schools.* Portsmouth, NH: Heinemann, 2006.
Glasser, W. *Choice Theory: A New Psychology of Personal Freedom.* New York: HarperCollins, 1998.
Graves, D. *Build a Literate Classroom.* Portsmouth, NH: Heinemann, 1991.
Jin, H. *Waiting.* New York: Vintage/Random House, 1999.
Kafalas, D. *Whale Pirates.* North Charleston, SC: Debut Press, 2002.

SELECTED BIBLIOGRAPHY

Keene, E., and S. Zimmerman. *Mosaic of Thought: Teaching Comprehension in a Reader's Workshop.* Portsmouth, NH: Heinemann, 1997.

Lane, B. *After the End: Teaching and Learning Creative Revision.* Portsmouth, NH: Heinemann, 1992.

Marzano, R. *A Different Kind of Classroom: Teaching with the Dimensions of Learning.* Alexandria, VA: Association for Supervision and Curriculum Development, 1992.

Murray, D. *A Writer Teaches Writing,* 2nd edition. Boston, MA: Thomson/Heinle, 2004.

National Commission on Writing. "The Neglected 'R': The Need for a Writing Revolution." New York: National Commission on Writing, 2003.

National Endowment for the Arts. "Reading at Risk: A Survey of Literary Reading in America." New York: National Endowment for the Arts, 2004.

Newsome, C. "A Teacher's Guide to Fair Use and Copyright: Modeling Honesty and Resourcefulness." http://home.earthlink.net/~cnew/research.htm. 1997.

O'Brien, T. *Going after Cacciato.* New York: Dell, 1975.

Parsons, L. *Response Journals.* Portsmouth, NH: Heinemann, 1990.

Paulsen, G. *Nightjohn.* New York: Bantam Doubleday, 1993.

Probst, R. *Response and Analysis: Teaching Literature in Junior and Senior High.* Portsmouth, NH: Heinemann, 1998.

Rowling, J. K. *Harry Potter and the Sorcerer's Stone.* New York: Scholastic Paperbacks, 1999.

Safier, Fannie, ed., *Adventures in Reading: Heritage Edition Revised.* Orlando, FL: Harcourt Brace Jovanovich, Inc., 1985.

Smith, F. *Joining the Literacy Club: Further Essays into Education.* Portsmouth, NH: Heinemann, 1988.

Tomlinson, C. A., and J. McTighe. *Integrating Differentiated Instruction and Understanding by Design.* Alexandria, VA: Association for Supervision and Curriculum Development, 2005.

Trubisz, S. "As a Writer I Can. . . ." In *The Portfolio Source Book,* ed. A. Green and B. Lane. Shoreham, VT: Vermont Portfolio Institute, 1994.

Weaver, C. *Reading Process and Practice: From Socio-Psycholinguistics to Whole Language.* Portsmouth, NH: Heinemann, 1988.

SELECTED BIBLIOGRAPHY

Webb, N. "Depth-of-Knowledge Levels for Four Content Areas." Wisconsin Center for Education Research. March 28, 2002.

Wilhelm, J. *"You Gotta Be the Book": Teaching Engaged and Reflective Reading with Adolescents.* New York: Teacher's College Press, 1997.

Wixson, K. K., and E. Dutro. "Standards for Primary Grade Reading: An Analysis of State Frameworks." *Elementary School Journal* 100 (1999): 89–110.

ABOUT THE AUTHOR

Dennis J. Kafalas, MA, is currently a high school principal. During his twenty-one years in the profession, he has worked in urban and suburban settings and has taught a variety of students in meaningful and insightful ways. He is a former member of the executive board of the Rhode Island Writing Project at Rhode Island College and is the author of an adult novel for young adults, *Whale Pirates* (Debut Press, 2002).

PERMISSIONS

Excerpt from *Go Ask Alice* by Anonymous reprinted with the permission of Simon & Schuster Books for Young Readers, an imprint of Simon & Schuster Children's Publishing Division. Copyright © 1971 Simon & Schuster, Inc.

Excerpt from *The Truth about Writing (Fiction)* by W. Appel, copyright 1997, reprinted with permission from Hastings House Publishers.

Excerpt from "As a Writer, I Can . . ." from *The Portfolio Source Book* by S. Trubisz, copyright 1994, reprinted with permission from Vermont Portfolio Institute and Discover Writing Press, www.discoverwriting.com.

Excerpt from *After the End* by Barry Lane, reprinted with permission. Copyright © 1992 by Barry Lane. Published by Heinemann, Portsmouth, NH. All rights reserved.

"Romeo and Juliet" excerpt from *Adventures in Reading: Heritage Edition Revised*, edited by Fannie Safier, copyright 1985, reprinted with permission from Harcourt Brace Jovanovich.

Excerpts from *Going after Cacciato* by Tim O'Brien, copyright 1978, and *Nightjohn* by Gary Paulsen copyright 1993, used with permission of Random House.

Excerpt from *Harry Potter and the Sorcerer's Stone* by J. K. Rowling. An Arthur A. Levine Book published by Scholastic Inc./Scholastic Press. Copyright © 1997 by J. K. Rowling. Reprinted by permission.

Excerpt from *Waiting* by Jin Ha, copyright 1999, reprinted with permission from Random House.

www.ingramcontent.com/pod-product-compliance
Lightning Source LLC
Chambersburg PA
CBHW021851300426
44115CB00005B/116